Exposing the call for Islamic Reformation

The Battle for Hearts and Minds

Adnan Khan

مكتبة اسلامية MaktabaIslamia

MaktabaIslamia Publications

www.maktabaislamia.com
info@maktabaislamia.com
www.facebook.com/everythingislamic
www.twitter.com/maktabaislamia

2016 CE – 1437 H

Translation of the Qur'ān

It should be perfectly clear that the Qur'ān is only authentic in its original language, Arabic. Since perfect translation of the Qur'ān is impossible, we have used the translation of the meaning of the Qur'ān throughout the book, as the result is only a crude meaning of the Arabic text.

Qur'ānic verses appear in speech marks proceeded by a reference to the Surah and verse number. Sayings (*Hadith*) of Prophet Muhammad ﷺ appear in inverted commas along with reference to the Hadith Book and its Reporter.

صلى الله عليه وسلم - ﷺ (Peace be upon him)

سبحانه وتعالى - ﷻ (Glory to Him, the Exalted)

CONTENTS

Introduction

The Italian Prime Minister, Silvio Berlusconi boasted after the events of 9/11:

"...we must be aware of the superiority of our civilisation, a system that has guaranteed well being, respect for human rights and - in contrast with Islamic countries – respect for religious and political rights, a system that has its values understanding of diversity and tolerance...The West will conquer peoples, like it conquered communism, even if it means a confrontation with another civilisation, the Islamic one, stuck where it was 1,400 years ago..."[1]

And in a 2007 report the RAND institute declared:

"The struggle underway throughout much of the Muslim world is essentially a war of ideas. Its outcome will determine the future direction of the Muslim world."

Building moderate Muslim Networks, RAND Institute

The concept of *'islah'* (reform) is a concept unknown to Muslims. It never existed throughout the history of the Islamic civilisation; it was never debated or even considered. A cursory glance at classical Islamic literature shows us that when the classical scholars laid the foundations of usul, and codified their Islamic rulings (*fiqh*) they were only looking to the comprehension of the Islamic rules in order to apply them. A similar situation occurred when the rules were laid down for the hadith, *tafseer* and the Arabic language. Scholars, thinkers and intellectuals throughout Islamic history spent much time understanding Allah's revelation – the Qur'an and applying the *ayaat* upon the realities and coined principals and disciplines in order to facilitate understanding. Hence the Qur'an remained the basis of study and all the disciplines that evolved were always based upon the Qur'an. Those who became smitten by Greek philosophy such as the Muslim philosophers and some from amongst the *Mut'azilah* were considered to have left the fold of Islam as the Qur'an ceased to be their basis of study. Thus for any Muslim attempting to deduce rules or understand what stance should be taken upon a particular issue the Qur'an is the basis of this study.

The first attempt at reforming Islam took place at the turn of the 19th century. By the turn of the century the Ummah had been in a lengthy period of decline where the global balance of power shifted from the Khilafah to Britain. Mounting problems engulfed the Khilafah whilst Western Europe was in the midst of the industrial revolution. The Ummah came to lose her pristine understanding of Islam, and in an attempt to reverse the decline engulfing the Uthmani's (Ottomans) some Muslims were sent to the West, and as a result became smitten by what they saw. Rifa'a Rafi' al-Tahtawi of Egypt (1801-1873), on his return from Paris, wrote a biographical book called *Takhlis al-ibriz ila talkhis Bariz* (The Extraction of Gold, or an Overview of Paris, 1834), praising their cleanliness, love of work, and above all social morality. He declared that we must mimic what is being done in Paris, advocating changes to the Islamic society from liberalising women to the systems of ruling. This thought, and others like it, marked the beginning of the reinventing trend in Islam.

Some even went as far as allowing foreign thoughts to be used as reference points alongside the Qur'an. Muhammad Abduh, the grand mufti of Egypt in 1899 is regarded as the founder of the so-called neomutazilim thinking.[2]

In his *tafseer* of the Qur'an he has the following to say:

"The abode of war (*dar al-harb*) is not a place for the establishment of the rules of Islam, therefore it is obligatory to make hijra unless there is an excuse or benefit for the Muslims due to which he will be safe from the *fitna* (test) on his *deen*. It is incumbent on the one who resides (in India) to serve the Muslims according to the best of his abilities and to strengthen the rules of Islam as much as he can. And there is no means of strengthening the influence of Islam and protecting the interests of the Muslims like the assuming of government posts especially if the government is lenient and fairly just between all nations and religions like the English government. It is well known that the laws of this country are closer to the Islamic *Shari'ah* more than others because it delegates most matters to the *Ijtihad* of judges. So whoever is qualified to be a judge in Islam and takes up a post in the judiciary in India with the correct aim and good intention, it is possible for him to do a great service for the Muslims."[3]

Abduh's most prominent disciples were Rashid Rida and Ali abd al-Raziq. Both students went on to write about the abolition of the Khilafah in 1924 and further reforms they felt necessary to strengthen Islam.

Hence the first attempts at reforming Islam resulted in the abolition of the Khilafah and the end of nearly fourteen centuries of Islamic rule. However with less then a century passing from this historical event Muslims have returned to Islam and every day edge closer to the re-establishment of the Khilafah. It is for this reason that the West has once again initiated plans to change Islam, since any revival of Islam will naturally end in the establishment of the Khilafah which represents an alternative system of governance that would then challenge the dominance of capitalism in the world.

The battle for hearts and minds is now fully underway. Former British Prime Minister Tony Blair outlined this after the 7/7 attacks in July 2005:

"It is not a clash of civilisations - all civilized people, Muslim or other, feel revulsion at it. But it is a global struggle. It is a battle of ideas and hearts and minds, both within Islam and outside."[4]

This battle is taking varying shapes and forms. A spectrum of various shades of modernist thought ranging from the extreme such as that of Irshad Manji to the more subtle such as Sheikh Ali Gomaa form part of this battle for hearts and minds. Amongst this spectrum are people from various backgrounds including academics, activists and traditional *Ulema*. All are in some shape or form, knowingly or unknowingly, propagating the reform of Islam in order to change Islam to fit with contemporary realities instead of working to change the reality in order to fit with Islam.

It is for this very reason this book has been written. To outline very clearly the attempts being undertaken to reform Islam and highlight the key styles and means being used. It outlines the specific arguments being used by the West and those smitten by the West. It looks at the events that have already occurred to reform Islam outlining the common approach taken by the West. It also outlines the correct method in defending Islam ensuring the responses do not inadvertently aid the agenda to reform Islam. It also outlines the method to go on the offensive rather than become defensive and accept the propaganda being levelled against Islam.

The battle for hearts and minds

It was after the events of 9/11 that the hatred for Islam by many in the West was paraded openly. The wars in Afghanistan and Iraq proved for many thinkers that Capitalism gained no currency in the Muslim world. In fact stories of Iraqi's welcoming US troops were found to be lies concocted by the US spin machine. Clearly it is no coincidence that the areas that are ultimately targets of the so-called 'war on terror' are Islamic countries with Muslim majority populations that could provide a base for future Islamic governance. These are the same countries where strategic resources - most notably oil and natural gas are concentrated. It is also no coincidence that both the 2002 and 2006 versions of the Pentagon's Quadrennial Review demonized Muslims, Islamic countries and Islam, in various guises, as grave threats to US security. The highest US officials were convinced that America's greatest ideological challenge is what they call 'a highly politicized form of Islam' and that Washington and its allies cannot afford to stand by and watch Muslims realise their political destiny, the Khilafah.

Lord Curzon, the British Foreign Minister at the time of the Khilafah's demise in 1924 announced to the House of Commons:

"We must put an end to anything which brings about any Islamic unity between the sons of the Muslims. As we have already succeeded in finishing off the Caliphate, so we must ensure that there will never arise again unity for the Muslims, whether it be intellectual or cultural unity."

This encapsulated how the superpower of the day viewed Islam as a threat to its very existence.

The fall of Communism in 1990 brought Islam into a direct clash with Capitalism. The former secretary general of NATO Willie Claes stated:

"The Alliance has placed Islam as a target for its hostility in place of the Soviet Union."

This led to a new onslaught against Islam. America has realised that cultural colonialism has not worked against the Muslims and now what is required is direct military colonisation. Paul Wolfowitz said at a press conference in Singapore:

"It's true that our war against terrorism is a war against evil people, but it is also ultimately a battle for ideals as well as a battle of minds."

The US national intelligence council published its report following its 'global 2020' project, entitled 'mapping the global future.' The National Intelligence Council (NIC) is the American intelligence community's centre for mid-term and long-term strategic thinking. The report set out the likely scenario the world will face in 2020. It concluded that the appeal of Islam today is a call to return to the earlier roots of Islam where the Islamic civilisation was at the forefront of global change under the Khilafah. Portraying a fictional scenario *'of how a global movement fuelled by radical religious identity could emerge,'*[6] the report revealed unequivocally that at the highest levels of US policy planning, preparation is being made for the emergence of the Khilafah. Other reports from US policy makers and think tanks across the world acknowledged there is a broad based ideological movement seeking the return of the Khilafah.

As a result senior policy makers including George W. Bush have 'warned' of the consequences of the Khilafah's re-establishment. Bush, in a speech to the American nation in October 2005 stated:

"The militants believe that controlling one country will rally the Muslim masses, enabling them to overthrow all moderate governments in the region, and establish a radical Islamic empire that spans from Spain to Indonesia."

On December 5th 2005, the then US Secretary of Defence, Donald Rumsfeld in remarks pertaining to the future of Iraq at John Hopkins University said:

"Iraq would serve as the base of a new Islamic Caliphate to extend throughout the Middle East and which would threaten the legitimate governments in Europe, Africa, and Asia. This is their plan. They have said so. We make a terrible mistake if we fail to listen and learn."

Tony Blair after 7/7 also referred to the need to confront an *"an evil ideology"* that included *"the establishment of effectively Taliban States and Shari'ah law in the Arab world en route to one Caliphate of all Muslim nations."* General David Petraeus, when asked about his priorities in the 'surge' operations in Iraq, in an interview with the Times published on June 20th 2007, said:

"It is to disrupt al-Qaeda and its ability to conduct sensational attacks and to try to continue the cycle of violence, which they have been trying to do all along. In addition, they are attempting try establish a real al-Qaeda sanctuary in Iraq, a caliphate."

These statements amongst numerous other arguments are being forwarded in an attempt to discredit and divert efforts towards the re-establishment of the Khilafah, particularly through seeking to associate it exclusively with terrorism. The effort has also been extended to malign the goals of Islamic politics more generally.

Thus alongside physical occupation, placing troops at strategic locations around the world and creating revolutions which are western friendly, a battle to win the hearts and minds of Muslims across the world is being fought. A suite of McCarthyite labels such as 'extremist', 'radical', 'fanatic' and 'militant' have become common currency in order to bring Muslims on side under the banner of a cultural war. Their definitions are dangerously loose and ever-broadening and manipulate the fact that there is no consensus on the definition of terrorism to brand Muslims as more prone to violence.

A consensus now exists across the Western world that a battle for hearts and minds needs to be fought and won otherwise more and more Muslims will turn to radicalism (Islam). In January 2007, Tony Blair's successor Prime Minister Gordon Brown, mentioned in regards to the Iraq war and 'terrorism':

"But you will not win against extreme terrorist activities and particularly the propaganda activities, unless you have this battle of hearts and minds that is won. And that makes me think of the same cultural war that had to be fought against communism from the 1940s and 50s onwards, is in a sense the model for what we've got to do here."[7]

The RAND institute published a report, 'Building Moderate Muslim Networks,' making a similar argument that the experience gained from supporting movements against the Soviet Union should be used as a template for the West to support networks of 'moderate' Muslims in order to counter, what they argue are, the radical and dogmatic interpretations of Islam that are gaining ground in the Muslim world.

The result of this led the US to develop a new plan in the battle for heats and minds.

In July 2003, the government's leading players in winning the 'war of ideas' against terrorism gathered at the National Defence University in Washington DC. There were crisis managers from the White House, diplomats from the State Department, and Pentagon specialists in psychological operations.

Washington's quick victory over Saddam Hussein's army that spring had done little to quell surging anti-Americanism overseas. Polls showed Osama bin Laden a more trusted figure than George W.Bush across the Muslim world including within US allies like Indonesia and Jordan.

After repeated missteps since the 9/11 attacks, the US government embarked on a campaign of political warfare unmatched since the height of the Cold War. From military psychological-operations teams and CIA covert operatives to openly funded media and think tanks, Washington was prepared to plough tens of millions of dollars into a campaign to influence not only Muslim societies but Islam itself. America realised it can no longer sit on the sidelines as radicals and moderates fight over the future of the Muslim world. The result has been a growing effort to influence what officials describe as an Islamic reformation.

The previously undisclosed effort was identified in the course of a four-month US News investigation, based on more than 100 interviews and a review of a dozen internal reports and memorandums. The investigation disclosed the various battles that were being fought or going to be initiated.

The CIA was revitalizing programs of covert action that once helped win the Cold War, targeting Islamic media, religious leaders, and political parties. The agency is receiving 'an exponential increase in money, people, and assets' to help it influence Muslim societies. Among the tactics are, working with militants at odds with al Qaeda and waging secret campaigns to discredit the worst anti-American zealots. The tools with which to fight back are varied. To the CIA, they are covert operations involving political influence and propaganda. At the Pentagon, they are called 'psyops' or strategic-influence efforts. At the State Department, they are called public diplomacy. All seek to use information to influence, inform, and motivate America's friends and enemies abroad. Many are controversial, particularly in light of recent revelations that administration officials have peddled fake video news reports and paid columnists to boost public perceptions of policies in the US. But to those toiling on the front lines against terrorism, the war of ideas and the tools to fight it are essential. How those tools have come back into use, and what Washington is doing with them, is a story that begins half a century ago, in the heyday of Soviet communism.

The White House has approved a classified new strategy, titled "Muslim World Outreach," which is a national security interest in influencing what happens within Islam. Because America is so hated across the Muslim world, the plan calls for working through third parties, moderate Muslim nations, foundations, and reform groups to promote shared values of democracy, women's rights and tolerance. The US has already quietly funded Islamic radio and TV shows, coursework in Muslim schools, Muslim think-tanks, political workshops and other programs that promote moderate Islam. Radio Sawa, a pop music-news station and Alhurra a satellite-TV news network have both been exposed as part of the US plan. Zeyno Baran, a terrorism analyst at the Nixon Centre said:

"You provide money and help create the political space for moderate Muslims to organize, publish, broadcast, and translate their work." She also says "the dilemma for Americans is that the ideological challenge of our day comes in the form of a religion—militant Islam, replete with its political manifestos, edicts, and armies."

On the eve of the US invasion of Iraq Deputy Defence Secretary Paul Wolfowitz said:

"We need an Islamic reformation, and I think there is real hope for one."

Daniel Pipes of the Philadelphia-based Middle East Forum (MEF), recently declared that the *"ultimate goal"* of the war on terrorism had to be Islam's modernisation, or, as he put it, *"religion-building."*

US aid is also finding its way to ensure US foreign policy aims are met. Working behind the scenes, State Department USAID now helps fund over 30 Muslim organizations across the Muslim world. Among the programmes are media productions, workshops for Islamic preachers, and curriculum reform for schools from rural academies to Islamic universities. One talk show on Islam and tolerance is relayed to radio stations in 40 cities and sends a weekly column to over a hundred newspapers. The grant list includes Islamic think-tanks that are fostering a body of scholarly research showing 'liberal' Islam's compatibility with democracy and human rights.

Another aspect of the strategy being pursued is to make peace with radical Muslim figures who eschew violence. At the top of the list is the Muslim Brotherhood, founded in 1928. Many brotherhood members, particularly in Egypt and Jordan, are at serious odds with al Qaeda. *"I can guarantee that if you go to some of the unlikely points of contact in the Islamic world, you will find greater reception than you thought,"* said Milt Bearden, whose 30-year CIA career included long service in the Muslim world. *"The Muslim Brotherhood is probably more a part of the solution than it is a part of the problem."* He confirmed that US intelligence officers have been meeting not only with sections of the Muslim Brotherhood but also with members of traditional Muslim movements in Pakistan; Cooperative clerics have helped dampen down fatwa's calling for anti-American jihad and persuaded jailed militants to renounce violence.

A Key aspect of the struggle is to reform Islam itself. However reform is unlikely to come from the Muslim world but rather from outside the Arab world. One solution being pushed is offering backdoor US support to reformers tied to Sufism, considered a tolerant branch of Islam.

The US is already funding Sufi Turkish religious leaders, leaders that oppose the State enforcement of Islamic law, believing that most Islamic regulations concern people's private lives and only a few on matters of governance. The State, they believe, should not enforce Islamic law, because religion is a private matter, and the requirements of any particular faith should not be imposed on an entire population. Fethullah Gülen asserts the compatibility of Islam and democracy and accepts the argument that the idea of republicanism is very much in accord with early Islamic concepts of shura. He holds that the Turkish interpretation and experience of Islam are different from those of others, especially the Arabs. He writes of an "Anatolian Islam" that is based on tolerance and that excludes harsh restrictions or fanaticism.[8]

Another aspect of the battle is the drive to develop a wedge between Muslims by dividing Muslims along lines of moderate and extremist. The RAND report 'civil democratic Islam' divided the Ummah into four camps; fundamentalists, traditionalists, modernists and secularists. The aim here is to work with the various moderate groups whilst isolating those that believe Islam is the solution. This includes the likes of the Nahdlatul Ulama an Institute for Islamic and Social Studies (LKiS) who hold that instead of creating specifically Islamic schools, Muslims should ensure that all institutions are infused with values of social justice and tolerance. The "i" in LKiS (which stands for Islam) is deliberately written in lower case to underscore that LKiS is against the type of Islamism that emphasizes Islam's superiority over other religions. LKiS is currently involved in human-rights training in pesantren,9 the Indonesian Islamic boarding schools.

The US has also sponsored Euro Islam Projects including a student initiative sponsored by the pro–European Union Students' Forum AEGEE. The group sponsors workshops, student exchanges, lecture events, and publications aimed at defining and promoting a specifically European, modern Islam that retains an Islamic character yet is open to the surrounding society.

Help has also been extended to modernists and secularists such as Bassam Tibi, who has a frequent presence on the European lecture circuit. As the founder of the Arab Organization for Human Rights and a member of several organizations that promote Muslim-Jewish and Muslim-Christian-Jewish dialogue. He is strongly supportive of the integration of Muslim minorities into mainstream European society and opposed to parallel legal, cultural and social systems. His outspoken belief is that immigrants should accept the values of the dominant Western culture (the Leitkultur) instead of attempting to subvert or change it. He also opposes what is called *Parallelgesellschaft* (Parallel Security). In this regard Tibi differs persistently and insistently with the Islamist premise that Islam is necessarily entwined with the public space and with politics; he opposes any inroads of Islamic law in Europe, arguing that *"the relationship between shari'ah and human rights is like that between fire and water."*[10]

The US Defence Department recognized in its Quadrennial Defence Review Report, that the United States is involved in a war that is *"both a battle of arms and a battle of ideas,"* in which ultimate victory can only be won *"when extremist ideologies are discredited in the eyes of their host populations and tacit supporters."*[11]

The National Security Strategy document of September 2002 elucidated a refined conception of security that emphasizes the consequences of internal conditions of other States particularly the lack of democracy. This theme was to be reinforced over the course of the next several years, from the 9/11 Commission Report to, perhaps most dramatically, President Bush's second inaugural address. From its prominence in a series of high-profile documents and speeches, the President's "Freedom Agenda" can be considered a US "grand strategy" in the Global War on Terrorism. The agenda identifies social sectors that would constitute the building blocks of the proposed reformation of Islam giving priority to liberal and secular Muslim academics and intellectuals, young moderate religious scholars, community activists, and Women's groups engaged in gender equality campaigns and moderate journalists and writers.

Understanding the battle for hearts and minds

The battle for hearts and minds is primarily being developed and fought in the West; this is because the authoritarian atmosphere in the Muslim world has ensured such discussions generally cannot occur. Also such a discussion is needed in the West to create a particular trend between Muslims and non-Muslims. The money and resources needed for potential conflicts in the Muslim world require justification to the people of the West. Hence disdain is being created for Islam; lies are being peddled against Islam that justifies prolonged military presence in the Muslim world. Such propaganda will then be exported to the Muslim world. A number of events have been used to justify to Western audiences that Islam is the new Communism that needs to be fought and destroyed. This propaganda is aimed at radicalising Western audiences against Islam as well as developing the type of resilience required for a 'long war'.

In December 2003 the Stasi commission proposed the banning of religious symbols in schools including the Hijab for the protection of secularism in France. The Stasi commissions were set up by the French president to research into the strength of secularism in France and propose policies to protect it. The proposal to ban religious symbols in schools was primarily aimed at Muslims, as the Muslims represented the largest minority in public schools. Such a proposal shocked all Muslims in Europe and caused much controversy and debate. The attacks on Islam, women and the woman's dress received ferocious vilification by the media and MP's across Europe. The image was portrayed that Muslims are separatist in Europe who do not integrate and adherence to the Hijab stands in the way if Muslims want to be considered part of Europe. The failure of France to convince Muslims of secularism and stamp out blatant racism and discrimination was blamed upon the existence of Islam.

In May 2004 Shabina Begum a student from Luton, UK, appealed in court when she was not allowed to wear the jilbaab in school. The claim was made on the grounds that the school had interfered with her right to manifest her religion and her right to education (both rights enshrined in the European Convention on Human Rights). Shabina Begum lost the case in the High Court, but later won on appeal to the Court of Appeal. The school appealed against this decision, and the case was heard by the Judicial Committee of the House of Lords who eventually ruled in favour of the school. The whole case caused much controversy and discussion in the UK due to the fact that the jilbaab manifestly represented Islam. Whilst child obesity, teenage pregnancies and knife crime occupied most news reporting in the UK many Muslims felt pressured to criticize Shabina Begum for taking her case to court as many non-Muslims felt this was an abuse of the freedoms afforded to citizens. Many Muslims in the UK argued modesty was the Islamic dress rather then the jilbaab. This event illustrated for many non-Muslims that the needs of Muslims cannot co-exist with liberal Britain thus Islam needs to be changed.

In 2005 Amina Wadud professor of Islamic studies at Virginia Commonwealth University lead the controversial Jummah prayer in New York which consisted of both men and women in the jamaat (congregation). Amina Wadud published a book in 1999 the *"Qur'an and Woman: Rereading the Sacred Text from a Woman's Perspective,"* which was the first feminist translation of the Qur'an. This incident led to much discussion on how Islam does not cater for women and projected the image that Islam oppresses women.

In September 2005 the Danish newspaper Jyllands-Posten published pictures of the Prophet Muhammad (saw) which led to demonstrations across the world, some protests turning violent. Many thinkers in the West argued that Capitalism allows the freedom to insult and Muslims should accept this as this is a Western tradition. Liberals argued Muslims demand a special position, insisting on special consideration for Islam. Flemming Rose Jyllands-Posten Culture editor was very open with his agenda he said *"his paper was not singling out Islam for attack, but was drawing Muslims into a secular fold."* [12] This controversy resulted in world-wide protests where some became violent, however the issue was successfully blamed on Muslims for feeling insulted and Muslims were criticized for violent demonstrations. Many Muslims feeling the pressure responded by condemning the actions of those demonstrating and condemning the imams who lead them and ostracizing them from being their representatives. This issue was successfully used to prove to Europe that Muslims wanted special status for Islam in secular societies.

In October 2006 Jack Straw, the UK's former foreign secretary, in an interview sparked controversy by commenting that he felt uneasy speaking to women who wear the Niqab (face veil). This incident was quickly used by the government and changed from a debate where an MP made offensive remarks about Islamic dress to *'women who wear veils over their face make community relations harder.'* [13] The then Prime Minister Tony Blair described the *niqab as a 'mark of separation'* [14] and thus debate began in the UK on why Muslims insist on wearing Islamic dress and the reasons for not integrating. One leading organisation commented that it understood Mr Straw's discomfort, and once again Islam was labeled as the problem causing further tensions between the Muslim community and the host country.

In February 2008 Rowan Williams, the Archbishop of Canterbury in the UK gave a speech in which he mentioned that the adoption of *Shari'ah* law *'seems unavoidable.'* Williams was later forced to comment further to defend himself as the media frenzy grew and the open questioning of Muslim loyalty was brought into question. Many argued that the *Shari'ah* is barbaric and made very clear there is only one law for every citizen in Britain hence

Muslims must show where their loyalty stands. The fact that a Christian bishop raised the discussion mattered little to Britain and the hatred for an essential element of Islam was paraded openly. This attack on Islam led to some Muslims condemning the Bishop as the UK supposedly has only one law, however many Muslims argued *Shari'ah* was only for the Muslim world and that there are many interpretations of *Shari'ah*.

The West has managed to draw upon many resources to attack Islam and facilitate the call for it to be reformed. Cherie Blair made her views very clear in a press conference in 2001:

"We all know that the Taliban is a regime that denies all its citizens even the most basic of human rights and for women that has been particularly acute. Things that women in our country take for granted, just to be able to enjoy life publicly with our families, to dress as we please. All of these things are forbidden. In Afghanistan if you wear nail polish, you could have your nails torn out. Well, that may seem a trivial example, but it is an example, nonetheless, of the oppression of women, and nothing more I think symbolises the oppression of women than the burkha which is a very visible sign of the role of women in Afghanistan and we had some interesting discussions about what it is like to wear a burkha and how difficult it makes just ordinary, everyday living…"[15]

Melanie Phillips has long called for the reformation of Islam. In 2002 she said:

"But the problem is that it (Islam) does not just oppose libertinism. Having never had a 'reformation' which would have forced it to make an accommodation with modernity, it is fundamentally intolerant and illiberal. As a result, it directly conflicts with western values in areas such as the treatment of women, freedom of speech, the separation of private and

public values, and tolerance of homosexuality. These are all liberal fundamentals and are not negotiable."[16]

And Salman Rushdie has long called for a reformation:

"What is needed is a move beyond tradition, nothing less than a reform movement to bring the core concepts of Islam into the modern age, a Muslim [Islamic] Reformation to combat not only the jihadist ideologues but also the dusty, stifling seminaries of the traditionalists, throwing open the windows to let in much-needed fresh air. It is high time; for starters, that Muslims were able to study the revelation of their religion as an event inside history, not supernaturally above it."[17]

Academics, journalists and politicians have on every opportunity called for Islam's reformation. This atmosphere has led many opportunists to take advantage of this climate for their own short term gains.

All of this collectively has led to a climate of fear pushing Muslims in Europe into a defensive posture and feeling uncomfortable in explaining Islam's stance on the various incidents. Some Muslims have unfortunately twisted Islam to make it more palatable to the West which has aided the call for a reformation.

Many Muslims who have been smitten by the West have for many years been calling for the abandonment of some aspects of Islam thus fulfilling the West's agenda. With minority relations drastically deteriorating since the bombings of Madrid and London, Europe abandoned policies which recognised Islam such as multiculturalism and began advocating the adoption of secular liberal values for minorities to co-exist in Europe. Coupled with anti-Hijab legislation across Europe, Muslims in Europe are being forced to change Islam as Islam is seen as backward and not compatible with secularism.

Tariq Ramadhan, regarded as a leading Islamic academic in the West, has long advocated reform and has been on the boards of many government programmes looking at the presentation of Islam in the West. The problem, according to Ramadhan, is with theologians who make rulings on certain subjects without having the worldly experience to do and, in the process mix traditional values with religion. Although his statements are usually unclear and ambiguous, there is no doubt that his views have been regarded by Westerners as a call for internal reform. In his 1999 publication he advocated that the geopolitical concepts of *dar ul-Islam and dar ul-kufr* were outdated and that *"Muslims are obliged to be loyal citizens and to influence the polity in constructive ways. Their goal should be to be in Europe but at home. To be a Muslim in Europe ideally means to interact with the whole of society. Ultimately, a European Islam should emerge, much as there already exists an African or Asian Islam."*[18] Ramadan in 2005 even called for a re-evaluation of Islam's punishment system.[19]

The intensity of the attacks on Islam led to some developing the *fiqh* of Minorities, which is a particular methodology where the Islamic rule can be changed due to the mere reason of residing in the West.

Much study and money by think tanks went into this project as this approach makes the particular reality faced, or the environment, the source of legislation. As a consequence certain rules will be neglected and this approach has led to the contradiction of established rules from the Qur'an and Sunnah. This *fiqh* has spawned a European Islam. Under the guise of intellectualism and re-opening the doors of *Ijtihad* many Muslim thinkers have justified many acts considered conclusively haraam in Islam. Such thinkers have completely misused terminology in order to justify the unjustifiable. For example, Irshad Manji openly supports homosexuality a well known prohibited act according to the Qur'an and Sunnah. She even proudly posted a photo of herself with gay and lesbian Palestinians in Jerusalem on her website.

Hence under the onslaught from the West and under pressure to make Islam palatable many Muslims and those who claimed to be Muslims, have changed Islam, aiding the West's call for reform. Scholars in the Muslim world have also not been spared in this effort. Such individuals are regularly invited to represent Muslims on government projects, conferences and even develop policies and legislation. Cambridge University organised one such event on 4th June 2007 on 'Islam and Muslims in the world today.' The grand Mufti of Egypt, Ali Gomaa, alongside many 'moderate' Muslims were invited to discuss how Islam can be changed to meet the needs of the West. Ali Gomaa responded by outlining how Islam had no political system: "Many assume that an Islamic government must be a caliphate, and that the caliph must rule in a set and specific way. There is no basis for this vision within the Islamic tradition. The caliphate is one political solution that Muslims adopted during a certain historical period, but this does not mean that it is the only possible choice for Muslims when it comes to deciding how they should be governed. The experience that Egypt went through can be taken as an example of this. The period of development begun by Muhammad Ali Pasha and continued by the Khedive Ismail was an attempt to build a modern state. This meant a reformulation of Islamic law. This process led Egypt to become a liberal state run by a system of democracy without any objections from Muslim scholars. Muslims are free to choose whichever system of government they deem most appropriate for them."[20]

The Grand Mufti went even further when he mentioned one could apostatize from Islam:

"The essential question before us is can a person who is Muslim choose a religion other than Islam? The answer is yes, they can, because the Qur'an says, *"Unto you your religion, and unto me my religion,"* (TMQ 109:6).[21]

When he was pressed on reversing such a stance his spokesman, Sheikh Ibrahim Negm, affirmed: "The mufti wrote this in a Western context," "Religion is a personal matter. People everywhere, including Egypt, are converting from one religion to another all the time and that is their business." "If a westerner, who has converted to Islam, for example, does not find satisfaction in Islam, then he is legally permitted to convert back. He is committing a major religious sin, however."[22]

Hence under certain circumstances, such as living in the West, it is permitted to abandon Islam according to Ali Gomaa. Some have even gone as far as to change the core tenets of Islam. Muhammad Nour Dughan a member of the scientific council of Istanbul University issued a fatwa in October 2007 reducing the five daily prayers to three. His justification was that Islamic law allows for the possibility of praying three times a day in cases of sickness or travel. He extended this option allowing Muslims to pray three times a day, especially when they are heavily committed with work or personal issues. The Turkish debate echoes a similar one that took place in Egypt where the fatwa also drew some support.

Essentially the call for an Islamic reformation is saying to Muslims all over the world that the Qur'an is a product of its time and place which reflects Muhammad's (saw) own experiences. The Qur'an is a historical document, which is now outdated and needs to be re-interpreted to suit the new conditions of successive new ages. Thus Islam is outdated and in its current form has no place in the world, thus it needs to be reformed, re-interpreted and changed to fulfil the conditions of the 21st century. Such an interpretation requires the Qur'an to be more in line with Western liberal standards. Only then will it be termed modern. Hence the call for Islamic reformation is a call for the re-interpretation of the Islamic texts to accord with the West.

A host of arguments have been presented justifying the re-interpretation of Islam. These can be summarized as:

- Islam can change from time and place, primarily because Imam Shafi did so with his *fiqh*.
- The claim that the *shari'ah* has remained silent on new issues and that the existing methodology of Islam is incapable of dealing with these issues.
- The claim that the Muqasid *–shari'ah* aim is to bring benefit to the people, so the *shari'ah* is where the benefit is.
- The Islamic world view of Dar ul-Islam and Dar ul-kufr needs changing as they are products of jurists, and not from the Islamic sources and are geopolitical terms only relevant to the time in which they were formulated.
- Using the *ahadith* as a source needs to be re-evaluated as they cannot be authentically proven.
- *Ijtihad* is Islam's tool of critical evaluation which allows varying opinion within Islam and this is the way forward to make Islam relevant.
- Difference of opinion (*uloom al Ikhtilaaf*) allows for liberal interpretations.

This debate and the subsequent response from Muslim scholars have left Muslims in a state of confusion. Does Islam need updating? Is it natural that Islam modernises in order to survive? The subsequent chapters will focus and review some of these arguments outlining their details and refuting their intellectual foundations.

The fallacy of Western universalism

The claim that Islam is backward and has no place in the world today is often built upon the premise that none of the Muslim countries have produced anything in terms of scientific research or technological development. It is often claimed that progress in science and technology occurred in the West when it rid itself of the authority of the Church and separated religion from life. Today this claim has become the criterion to study any alternative thought. Thus when Muslims are questioned about their views on homosexuality or apostasy the question essentially being asked is: do you believe in the universal views on such issues delineated by secularism? Many Muslims have fallen into the trap. Often through sincerely trying to defend Islam, of presenting Islam as agreeing with secular liberalism, this being the default standard by which all thoughts are measured.

An example of this was when a leading Muslim leader in the UK was asked, *should Muslim women have to wear the veil, niqab or burqa?* He answered *"No one should be compelled to wear either the hijab (headscarf), the niqab (face-veil) or the burqa (full body covering). [But] Islam calls upon both men and women to dress modestly."*[23]

The question essentially being asked is: do Muslim women have the freedom NOT to cover? Here the Islamic rule was presented in order to agree with freedom of expression, a Western ideal. This is one of the founding arguments of Islamic reformation that Islam is at odds with the universal values of Liberalism which render it outdated and deserving of reform similar to what happened to the reformation of the Christian church.

The historical process the West underwent is considered the history of the world and termed modernity, whilst all alternative thoughts are primitive if they do not match Western Liberalism (Capitalism). There are however some fundamental differences between the history of the West and the struggle with the Church, relative to Islam and its history that clouds the judgment when ascertaining the validity of Islam. In order to understand this we need to understand the history of the West.

The initial adoption of Christianity by the Roman Empire was not based on the legitimacy of Christianity or on its ability to deal holistically with humanity's affairs. Rather, Christianity was adopted by Constantine in 325 CE simply to preserve the Empire by building a common mentality and loyalty among citizens. Christianity offered blind loyalty to the secular emperors based on the understanding that society could have two separate authorities; one temporal, the other spiritual, and that both authorities could coexist harmoniously. This understanding came from the saying attributed to Jesus (AS):

"Render unto Caesar what is Caesar's and unto God what is God's." The Bible - NKJ Version (Luke 20:25)

Despite this, Christianity could not sustain or preserve the Empire and the demise of the Romans as a force meant the Church was able to dominate much of Europe. The domination of the Church meant that all affairs of life had to conform to the dogma of the Church. This caused countless problems given that the Bible, which the Church used as its authoritative text, dealt with only very limited matters. The scope of the Bible, as the Church would be the first to admit, does not and cannot stretch to being used wholly and exclusively to govern a nation or civilisation. Even determined advocates of the Bible fully accept it cannot be the primary source for the derivation of detailed rules, prescripts and guidance on every issue humanity faces till the Last Day. It did give some specific rules related to the Jews in their worships and their foodstuffs. It gave general moral principles for Christians and set norms for their prayers and communal worship. It did not give detailed regulation and direction on economy, accession to ruling, foreign policy, transactions, leasing of land, contracts, representation, judiciary, criminal punishments, the structure, accountability and functioning of government etc.

This meant there was a huge gap in the political landscape and this was an area of constant conflict of interests between kings, feudal barons and priests. During Europe's dark ages it was the priests who dominated life and when they passed judgement all had to submit, even Kings. Yet the judgements of priests were an arbitrary and inconsistent exercise of their authority owing to the lack of comprehensive legislative texts to base their rules upon. It was this essentially random practice that laid the seeds of direct confrontation between the Church and society. With the passage of time scientific discoveries were made that were at odds with the teachings of the Church. To preserve its authority, the Church took harsh steps against the emergence of such new ideas. Scientists were branded as heretics, infidels and Satan's. In 1633 CE, Galileo was forced to renounce his belief and writings that supported the Copernican theory of heliocentrism that claimed the Earth circumvented the Sun. Instead, the Church adamantly maintained the flawed theory of geocentricism, which stated that the Sun circumvented the Earth. Other thinkers, such as Bruno, suffered even worse treatment at the hands of the Church. Bruno was imprisoned for 8 years while questioning proceeded on charges of blasphemy, immoral conduct, and heresy. Bruno was eventually burned at the stake.

Also, plenty of evidence exists indicating that hundreds of thousands of women, alleged to be witches were brutally tortured, burnt and drowned. The response to this oppression from the people, especially the scientists, thinkers and philosophers was equally strong. Many began to highlight the contradictions of the Church and reformers such as Martin Luther and John

Calvin called for nothing less than the complete separation of the Church from the State. Desperate measures were taken by the Church to deflect the people's criticism, frustration and anger but these measures failed to halt the flames of change that had galvanised the masses. The Church realised that it could no longer remain dominant without reform. The eventual outcome of the struggle for power between the Church, on the one hand, and the scientists, thinkers and philosophers, on the other, was the complete separation of the Church from State. This compromise solution limited the authority of the Church to preserving morals in society and conducting rituals. It left the administration of worldly affairs to the State itself. The Reformation led to the Enlightenment period that bred secularism as a worldview and finally removed the arbitrary authority of the Christian Church. This formed the basis of the Capitalist ideology and sparked the industrial revolution in Europe.

This state of affairs led to an intense intellectual revolution in Europe. European philosophers, writers and intellectuals made considerable efforts for comprehensive change in European ideas with the aim of uniting Europeans under secular liberal democratic thought i.e. Capitalism. Many movements were established and played a great part in the emergence of new opinions about life. One of the most significant events that occurred was the change of the political and legislative systems to the nation state. The spectre of a despotic monarchy gradually disappeared to be replaced by republican systems based on representative rule and national sovereignty. This had the effect of triggering the awakening of Europe from its slumber. The industrial revolution was the centre of the European scene. There were numerous scientific discoveries and inventions springing from Europe. These factors all boosted Europe's intellectual and material progress. This material and scientific progress resulted in Europe finally riding itself of its medieval culture.

When Europe rid itself of the Christian Church, science and technology came to flourish. Today, advocates of secularism claim Islam needs to go through a reformation process similar to the West whereby Muslims redefine and confine Islam to individual worship rather then a political creed i.e. do away with *Shari'ah*, Khilafah, jihad, hudood (punishments) and adopt allegedly universal values of secularism, freedom, democracy, Human Rights, pluralism and the rule of law. The unfounded claim is that only with such reform Muslims can progress and make a transformation just as the West has done.

This understanding is flawed due to two reasons:

- Liberal thinkers saw Christianity as folklore as well as being part of their cultural heritage. This led them to deny miracles, revelation, prophets and other religious beliefs. This was because for them the Christian creed, which all these ideas and beliefs were based upon, was diametrically opposed to rationality.

- For Western thinkers the Church and enlightened thought cannot meet. Martin Luther the famous Christian reformer said,

"Among Christians the rule is not to argue or investigate, not to be a smart aleck or a rationalistic know-it-all; but to hear, believe, and persevere in the Word of God, through which alone we obtain whatever knowledge we have of God and divine things. We are not to determine out of ourselves what we must believe about him, but to hear and learn it from him." (LW. 13.237; Q. in Wood, 120).

This means Christianity is not based on intellectual thought, rather even if the scripture contradicts the clear mind, the scripture must always take precedence.

Defining all religions like Christianity and Islam as in the dark ages is a disservice to critical debate. It deflects any potential debate on secular liberal values and demonstrates clear insincerity in discussing which way humanity should move forward.

The history and struggle of the West was an event that occurred in Europe and was not the only event taking place in the world. When secularists study Islam, they view it through the lens of their history, which was their struggle to remove the authority of the church. For them Islam is no different to the church - irrational, medieval etc, and therefore it needs a reformation, just as the Christian Church went through. Only then can Islam be considered to have met the criteria for modernity.

Thus for the West 'modernity' carries specific connotations of the Enlightenment mission, defined as emancipation from self-imposed infancy i.e. from religion. This mission resulted in the development of secularism and the banishing of the Church, its teachings and its dogma to the private sphere. This was in addition to human rights, equality and freedom. Soon this historical process was termed 'modernism'. For secularists, the adoption of secular liberal values is termed modern and anything not compatible with such values is backward and no different to the medieval Church.

What is being discussed here is an alternative ideology and an alternative way of organising life's affairs to the current secular model. There exists some fundamental differences between the two models – the secular and Islamic models are not the same. They do not overlap as they do not stem from the same fundamental ideas. They will therefore have entirely different impressions on how society should look. These differences lead to each viewing the other as a potential challenger to its superiority. Since secularism and Islam do not agree at the basis it is wholly inappropriate to judge this alternative using the secular model as a benchmark. Doing so would inevitably lead to the elimination of any methodology not in agreement with secularism before the discourse even commenced. No debate on secularism would ever take place!

If Islam is an alternative way to organise life it will inevitably have solutions which are the complete opposite to the secular model. However a non-agreement with the secular basis is not proof in itself to render a thought invalid. Consider the following:

- Would we consider the development of China wrong because it was not entirely built upon the free market model, even though it's on course to become the largest economy on the planet within 30 years?

- Would it be wrong for Indian companies to offer free medical alternatives to its poor because Capitalism abhors state intervention in the economy?

- Would it be correct for one to say the UK's fiscal policy is wrong because it does not have Islamic taxation incorporated into them?

- Would we consider state handouts to the poor wrong because Capitalism advocates leaving the wellbeing of citizens to the market?
What must also be agreed is that time alone is not enough to render a thought invalid; this is because ideas are never time specific. The revival of ancient Greek philosophy, art and culture was termed a renaissance in 16th Century Europe. Most of the legislation we find today across Western Europe has their traditions in writings three millennia old, which are still considered valid today. For example:

▪ The US Bill of Rights, passed in 1791, reflects the guarantee of due process which was taken from the Magna Carta in 1215.

▪ Western scholars and jurists study the thoughts of Aristotle, Plato, Machiavelli, Locke and Nietzsche with no qualms that these people lived a long time ago.

▪ Modern civil law was developed upon the theory of liability which has its origins in Roman law.

▪ Common law, which is the principle of deciding cases by reference to previous judicial decisions has its origins in the Middle Ages in Roman law and influenced by Norman Saxon custom. Today it remains a source of legislation for the UK, US and Canada.

From this perspective democracy would definitely be backward and primitive due to its ancient origins. So the fact Islam emerged in seventh century Arabia is not an argument to suggest modern inapplicability.

Capitalism's universality in reality is a Western specific ideology, an event which cannot be used to measure alternative thoughts as it is not a neutral measure. So it would be incorrect to place Islam on the West's political spectrum as this is a Western construct which follows their historical process.

The terms 'left' or 'right' derive from the seating positions in the National Assembly arising out of the 1789 French Revolution. The revolutionary groups sat on the Left and the conservative groups sat on the Right. These terms have come to be used relatively to compare between different factions and attitudes to state intervention. However wherever one sits on the political spectrum secularism forms their basis. So although there may have been numerous groups or sects in the history of Islam such as the mu'tazilah, jabriyah, khawarij, qa'dariyah, itnah ashari, the ashari, and ahul Sunnah, Islam formed their basis and it would be incorrect to speak about a Muslim left or term certain radicals as the Muslim right. This would only aid the integration of Islam with Capitalism thus aiding the reformation of Islam. The RAND report 'civil democratic Islam' proposed this method of reforming Islam by segmenting the Muslim into moderates, fundamentalists and liberals. Thus interpreting Islam from a Western perspective is in reality aiding the call for an Islamic reformation.

Islam is valid for all times and places

The call for reform fundamentally rests on the argument that Islam is not valid for all times and places, so new ideas need to be inserted into Islam and old ideas from the Islamic sources require changing and updating. A number of so called Islamic arguments are used such as Imam Shafi changing his *fiqh* when he travelled between Iraq and Egypt and various other instances at the time of the Prophet (saw). Essentially the argument for reform is that Islam is unable to deal with all the issues that humanity faces due to the Islamic sources being a product of history. What needs to be explored is: does Islam have the ability to deal with all issues comprehensively for all times and ages? If this is the case then the discussion of changing Islam becomes irrelevant.

This discussion however needs to be put in its correct context in order to be productive. The discussion is not on the standard of living in the Muslim world or in terms of scientific or technological elevation. Neither is the discussion about the fact that the *Shari'ah* needs to correspond to opinions advocated by Capitalists or even that progress is solely whatever corresponds to Western legislation. Whilst the situation in the Muslim world is clearly declined, it is imperative we understand from the outset the difference between a Muslim country and an Islamic one. No countries are Islamic at present since none of them implement Islam. Rather some apply a few rules of Islam but never in any of the major policies of the country. The examination of Muslim countries that leads to some of them being labelled Islamic is incorrect. Using these pseudo-Islamic States to determine whether Islam itself is compatible with the modern age would also be incorrect.

The crux of the argument is whether Islam is modern rather than if it concurs with modernity. For something to be modern it needs to be applicable for all times and ages rather then just agree with secular liberal values. Islam is not part of modernity in this sense since its values; intellectual basis and viewpoint of life differ from the secular basis. Therefore the Islamic legislation - the *Shari'ah* and the basis on which it is established needs to be studied in order to ascertain whether Islam is suitable to solve the problems of every age and remain consistent with its own unique basis, without deviation.Only then can the validity of Islam as being modern be measured fairly.

What is required is that the correct questions are asked such as:

-   Is Islamic legislation fit to be a field of thought such that it is possible to deduce rules for all types of relationships from its evidences, be they economic or social relationships?

- Does Islamic legislation have a wide spectrum of generalisations so that it is possible for its finite number of sources to encompass new and diverse issues?

-   Can collective principles and general thoughts be deduced?

-   Does Islam have the capacity to deal with the differences between people from different backgrounds, customs, nationalities and ideas creating cohesive and stable communities?

To prove the validity of Islam as being modern, new issues need to be examined and the Islamic texts studied in order to determine the possibility of deducing solutions, rules and principles from these texts for any issue that arises. This is the only productive basis of discussion and we should proceed in such a manner.

For legislation to be suitable for all ages, peoples and generations it should have the ability to offer solutions for any problems human beings face in any time and in any country. There should be no deviation from the intellectual basis of the legislation. If such deviation exited then this would demonstrate that the initial basis is not fit to derive legislation from.

An example of such an inconsistency is what occurred in English jurisprudence in the nineteenth century. Contract theory from Civil Law was defined as an agreement between two individuals that generates liability. This meant that a contract was between two (or more) people including an offer and acceptance. However, this understanding was eroded by the building of contracts solely upon the solidarity of a group (e.g. including Co-operatives, Partnerships and Public Limited Companies (PLCs) rather than the will of the individuals involved. The theory of liability deviated further with the introduction of the Solitary Will when stock markets came into existence. The Solitary Will is where an individual agrees to the written constitution of a company by purchasing its shares with no formal offer from anyone. This came to be termed as the Individual Will whereby shares could be exchanged very quickly without the need for two people to continuously come together and have a formal offer and acceptance. An example of this is the take-over bid of the world's richest football club, Manchester United FC by Malcolm Glazier. He imposed his will on the company (i.e. he brought shares) and even though other shareholders were against such an action it was a valid form of acquiring ownership from a jurisprudential angle even though there was only one person in the contract (acceptance but no offer). Both these examples are in clear contradiction to the initial Theory of Liability that did not permit such a contract. The initial basis had to be abandoned in the face of new developments thereby establishing its inadequacy.

Sociologists and psychologists such as Weber, Durkheim and Freud after studying empirical evidences could never reach solid consensus on what the human problems were. During their respective times they concluded these problems were far ranging from fear, earning of wealth, procreation, survival and worship etc. Some of these problems are instincts that we know already exist whilst others are still to be found and require incorporation into the body of study when discovered. This was their attempt at looking at the reality of humans in order to define the human problem. The context of this discussion is looking at the reality of the human being; therefore we are looking at the human being regardless of time and place as there is no difference between humans today compared to fourteen centuries ago as well as to the human twenty centuries into the future. Human needs and instincts remain the same regardless of external factors. These instincts are an unalterable reality that has existed since the time of the first man, Adam (aliys salam) i.e. this has always been the case. We can see that men and women find themselves attracted to the opposite sex and that they have maternal and paternal desires. People throughout the ages have always worshipped something, be it the Creator or something else such as a philosopher, a pop star, a ruler, a superhero, fire, a volcano or a planet. This again is an unalterable part of the human make-up that has never changed no matter whether the mode of transport was the camel or a plane. No one can claim to have two brains, four livers, or three hearts. Likewise they cannot claim to possess instincts other than procreation, survival and reverence. The fundamental point remains therefore that no matter what epoch or region is considered, humans are fundamentally the same, with the same instincts, needs and desires, irrespective of any other considerations.

Islam views the human being as composed of instincts and needs continually facing problems in how to satisfy them. This means the human problems are the same and never actually change. This is because what changes throughout time are the manifestations of instincts and not the instinct themselves. So we will not invent new instincts or a fourth instinct but rather they will remain as these three until the end of time, although over the course of one's life the manifestation may change. So one may change their religion, change which gender they feel attracted to or even decide there are certain commodities they will not buy due to their effect on the environment but one will still worship something, become sexually agitated and seek some form of possession.

What needs to be understood is that the Islamic texts came to address men and women as human beings, not just as individuals living in the seventh century Arabian Desert. The Islamic texts did not address humanity in relation to a particular time or place, but rather addressed humanity whether we were living a century ago, today, or in a 100 years time. The simple issue remains that a human living today is the same human who lived 1400 years ago and will continue to be the same human in another 1400 years time. Some verses in the Qur'an elaborate on this reality:

"You will not find in the creation of Allah any alteration."　　(TMQ Al-Fatir: 43)

The human whom Allah (swt) addressed 1400 years ago when it was said:

"Allah has permitted trade and forbidden usury."　　(TMQ Al-Baqarah: 275)

Is no different to a human addressed by the same speech today. One can see that the human whom Allah (swt) addressed more than 1000 years ago when it was said:

"Kill not your children for fear of want: We shall provide sustenance for them as well as for you: verily the killing of them is a great sin." (TMQ Al-Israa: 31], is no different to humanity today. And indeed when the Messenger Muhammad (saw) said:

"The son of Adam has no better right than that he would have a house wherein he may live and a piece of cloth whereby he may hide his nakedness and a piece of bread and some water"   (Tirmidhi)

He (saw) was of course not only referring to the needs of the Bedouins of Arabia.

So if we haven't changed and the Islamic texts that address us haven't changed, then what is so different today? Clearly the world is radically different from the one where Islam emerged and progressed in. The lifestyles of people nowadays are different to those of a century ago. However, what is clear is the nature of the problems that humanity faces have not changed. They are the same problems that have existed from the very creation of humanity, life and the universe. What have changed are the tools humans use to solve these problems. A few examples follow to illustrate this point.

In the past people would live in huts and today we have skyscrapers, but we still need houses and roofs over our heads. In the past Muhammad (saw) sent messengers to other rulers on horseback whereas today a message could be sent via e-mail, IM, fax or SMS. Muhammad (saw) and his companions fought many battles using horses, bows and arrows whereas today wars are still fought, but using 'Smart' technology, cruise missiles and satellite intelligence. In the past Muslims learnt astronomy so they could locate the Qibla wherever they went whereas today an electronic watch will do the same.

The fundamental point illustrated through these examples is that humans, with respect to their needs, are the same and the problems that they face have not changed. Any change that we perceive is merely a change in the tools or the devices that humans use when solving their problems.

The obvious point which follows on from this is that since the Islamic texts deal with humans and their problems, and not the tools that are used to solve their problems, the Islamic *Shari'ah* is as relevant to humanity today as it was when it elevated the people of Arabia. As a result one cannot claim Islam needs to be reformed or modernised to fit with modern life or adapt to modern life.

With regards to specific solutions to problems it needs to be understood firstly that Islamic legislation does not proceed upon the route taken by western legislation. It does not make freedom the subject of discussion, whether in affirming or negating it. Rather Islam makes the actions of human beings the fundamental subject of discussion. Islamic legislation has come to give guidance regarding the actions of human beings. It did not come to recognise or reject freedom. It does not look at humans from the angle of undertaking or not undertaking actions on the basis of freedom. Instead, Islam considers that actions are a result of humans wanting to satisfy their instincts and needs; therefore it's necessary to know their rules.

The *Shari'ah* can address an issue in a general manner which means the rule comes with a general meaning of defined description like:

"...and Allah has permitted trade" (TMQ Al-Baqara: 275).

Here the purchase or sale has not been restricted to a certain amount. The *Shari'ah* can also come in a specific manner where it can only be applied upon a reality and nothing more. Thus the verse for trade:

"Allah permitted trade and forbade riba (interest)" (TMQ Al Baqara: 275)

is originally of general import where all types of trade and transactions have been permitted but transactions involving interest have specific evidences which restrict the general rule, therefore they do not fall under the general rule. Otherwise Islamic legislation would just be full of lists of fruit, vegetables and other items with the appropriate ruling next to them explaining allowed or not allowed.

If something is not allowed it would be mentioned in name or description, and that what is allowed would be mentioned generally rather then listing all the permissible things. Thus Islam permitted the exchange of fruit, cars, chocolate as well as clothes. All these things fall under the original general ruling of trade, however the trade in certain goods such as pork, alcohol and drugs has specific evidences that exempt them from the general rule of permissibility.

Economics

With respect to the survival instinct, men and women will undertake a number of actions to survive. These range from the buying of food, taking ownership of property, selling goods, investment, agriculture, taking loans, exchanging currency, taking up employment and giving work, setting up a company, importing and exporting abroad, disposing of assets etc. In this regard, Islam made a distinction between the economic system and economic science i.e. it views them as two separate issues. This is because there is a fundamental difference between the method of production of goods and services (economic science) from the manner of their distribution (economic system).

The production of goods and services follow no particular viewpoint in life. A steel mill is neither Capitalist, Islamic nor Communist, therefore it is Universal. Questions as to how processes can be made more technological, how machinery and robots can improve productivity and how inventions can improve the process of manufacturing do not follow any specific viewpoint in life.

This means basic facts on productivity; marketing and manufacturing (economic science) remain the same irrespective of belief or location. This is similar to scientific facts. These are the same whether in China or the US because they are not influenced by any belief. They are questions based upon the reality i.e. understanding the reality at hand leads one to a conclusion. So the fact inflation occurs when there is too much money chasing too fewer goods does not change if one is a Christian or if an atheist becomes Muslim or if one move's from China to the US. This is no different to the fact that wood burns whatever your religion or whether you are in the UK or the North Pole.

The manner of distribution of resources, how goods and services should be given to the public, whether they should go to the rich or the orphans, aristocracy or the landlords etc. is not a discussion upon the reality i.e. understanding the reality at hand does not lead one to a conclusion. That which defines how to distribute the wealth, how to possess it, and how to spend or dispose of it (economic system) can never be taken from the reality as the reality does not explain this. The goods and what they are made of do not manifest themselves with answers of who they should go to. There is no indication simply from looking purely at the goods and services themselves of any way of deciding how they should be distributed. Therefore the answer must emanate from something external to the reality i.e. a belief system or ideology.

Islam does not view the human as an economic unit and then look to find the most economically viable solution thus viewing all problems, whether from marriage to pensions to drugs to education, from the angle of the economic effect and cost. Neither does Islam view the human the way the Communists did which is that people are simply matter, just one aspect of nature, nothing more. Islam views the human as being composed of organic needs as well as instincts, all of which requires answers on how to satisfy them. So Islam organised these instincts and needs in a way that ensures their satisfaction such as the needs of the stomach and the need to reproduce and others. However, this organisation is not arranged in Islam by satisfying some of them at the expense of others, nor by suppressing some of them, setting others loose, or setting all of them loose. Instead, Islam has co-ordinated the satisfaction of all of them in a way to ensure comfort, preventing conflicts and a lapse to a primitive level through the anarchism of instincts.

Via its own economic system, Islam laid down rules for the means to acquire wealth and commodities, how they can be utilised and their manner of disposal. It certainly did not make freedom of ownership the basis of the economic system or even the Marxist principal of 'from each according to his ability, to each according to his needs'. It did not define the basic problem as 'unlimited wants, limited resources'. Islam viewed the resources to be ample enough to completely satisfy the basic needs of all. Therefore, amongst a host of other detailed rules, one will find the *Shari'ah* aims to secure the satisfaction of all basic needs (food, clothing and housing) completely for every citizen of the Islamic State.

Islam defined the manner by which humans acquire wealth to prevent a minority of the populace from controlling the majority of the wealth so that the majority of people are not deprived of satisfying some of their needs. Via *Qiyas* (Analogical deduction) the following verse in the Qur'an ensures this situation never arises:

"That it (i.e. the nations wealth) does not become a commodity between the rich among you." (TMQ Al-Hashr:7)

This verse was discussing the issue of the rich receiving wealth and addressed the Khalifah to ensure the wealth is not distributed in a manner where it remains amongst the rich alone.

The Islamic economic system is built upon three principles:
1. Ownership
2. Disposal of ownership
3. The distribution of wealth amongst the people

In order to facilitate the acquisition of goods and services Islam put forward rules related to the manner of possessing wealth without any complications. Islam defined the legal means of ownership, and it defined the contracts through which possession can take place. This left humanity free to develop the styles and means by which they earn, as Islam did not interfere in the production of wealth.

Islam defines the legal means of ownership and contracts through general guidelines that include legal principles and rules, under which numerous issues belong and against which numerous rules are measured by Qiyas.

Thus Islam allowed employment, detailed its rules and left the person to work as a manufacturer, technician, trader, investor etc. Employment was legislated in such a way that by Qiyas it also includes representation. This is because the employee represents the employer of the company and is entitled to a salary. Gifts are legislated as a legal means of ownership and by Qiyas this can be extended to include donations, grants, charity and rewards as means of ownership. Thus in Islam the means of ownership and the contracts are detailed by the *Shari'ah* in general outlines and set in such a way as to include any contemporary incident.

Islam confined possession to particular means and as a result of this fact ownership came to be defined by the *Shari'ah* as the possession of goods, services and wealth according to divine means as permitted by the Lawgiver.

The *Shari'ah* has determined the means of ownership by specific cases which it made clear in a limited, rather than unrestricted form. The *Shari'ah* has laid down these means in clear general guidelines. These comprise of numerous sections, which are branches of these means and clarifications of their rules. The *Shari'ah* did not characterise the means by certain general criteria, so no other general means can be included through Qiyas. Islam allowed the work of an individual in return for a salary as this is considered as a legal means of ownership and the core condition for this is that he would be compensated for the effort by being paid a salary for the work. Islam allows the cultivation of land, its farming as well as what is known as agriculture. It allowed the extracting of what is in or on the earth, which means mining, exploration as well as construction. Under this general guideline you also have hunting, brokerage as well as sharecropping. Each of these sections can be extrapolated further by Qiyas.

By looking at the divine rules from the *Shari'ah* that allows humans to possess property, it becomes apparent that the means of possession in Islam are limited to five which are:

1. Work
2. Inheritance
3. Obtaining wealth for the sake of life
4. The State granting wealth to the citizens

5. Wealth and commodities that individuals take without exchange (gifts, donations and the like)

It cannot be claimed that Islam is restrictive and hinders economic activity because it has rigid rules which cannot evolve with time as economic activity increases and changes via the invention of new technologies. This is because humans want to own things in order to survive. Islam clarified which of these means can and cannot be utilised and many of these means can be applied and extended to new realities via Qiyas. The ownership of things will increase, decrease and diversify therefore its not necessary that new transactions and contracts be required as the issue at hand is which five means of possession are acceptable to acquire such things. The means to acquire have been laid down and as discussed earlier can be used forever, as they are not time specific.

Islam, men and women

The social system in Islam came to regulate the relationships between men and women. It organized the procreational instinct in a manner that does not lead to the neglect of other instincts nor suppress the procreational instinct in any manner.

The procreation instinct can be satisfied in many ways other than with the opposite sex. However, such attempts at satisfaction will not serve the purpose of civilisational continuance for which the instinct has been created in humanity except in one case that is if a man satisfies it with a woman and a woman satisfies it with a man. So the relationship of a man with a woman from the angle of instinctual sexuality is a natural relationship free from any abnormality in the eyes of Islam. It is the only relationship by which the survival of the human race is maintained. However, allowing this instinct to run loose would be detrimental to humanity and societal life. The outright promiscuity and sickening figures for sexual assault, paedophilia and rape in Europe are testimony to this.

The purpose of the procreational instinct in Islam is to produce offspring for the survival of the species. Therefore, the Islamic view of this instinct is oriented towards the survival of the species without distinction between men or women. Islam views the pleasure and enjoyment that is obtained by such satisfaction a natural and inevitable matter whether humanity considers it or not. This is the way Islam views the instinct and it laid down rules for both men and women upon this basis:

"It is He Who has created you from a single person, and He has created from him his wife, in order that he might enjoy the pleasure of living with her. When he had sexual relations with her, she became pregnant and she carried it about lightly. Then when it became heavy, they both invoked Allah, their Lord: If You give us a good child, indeed we shall be amongst the grateful."   (TMQ Al- Araf: 189)

In this Qur'anic verse the basis of the procreational instinct is confirmed i.e. the preservation of the human race. Islam restricted sexual relations i.e. the male-female relations between the man and woman to marriage only. Any relation outside of this is considered a crime and has a punishment prescribed. The other kinds of relations which are external manifestations of the procreation instinct, such as parenthood, childhood, brotherhood, uncle hood, are allowed and considered of the unmarriageable kinship. Islam permitted matters for women that it allowed for men such as practising trade and industry, agriculture, seeking knowledge, praying, engaging in politics etc.

Islam made co-operation between men and women in life's affairs and in the people's relations among themselves a fact in all dealings. This is seen from the following verses from the Qur'an that makes no distinction between males and females:

"Fasting is prescribed upon you." (TMQ Al-Baqarah: 183)

, and

"Establish the prayer." (TMQ Al-Anam: 72)

, and

"Sadaqat (alms) is only for the poor and the needy" (TMQ At-Tauba: 60)

These verses, amongst others, have come in the general form i.e. they apply to both men and women without differentiation between them. At the same time Islam mandated certain precautions against anything that would lead to an illegal sexual relationship or divert men and women from the specific system mandated to control the sexual relationship. Islam is very strict in observing these precautions. Thus, it made chastity outside of marriage mandatory. This is in addition to obliging the use of every method, style or means that would lead to the protection of chastity and morals.

Sanctification

An explanation of the sanctification instinct and the need to worship is inherently a discussion on the relationship between the created and the Creator. Although today many things and objects are viewed as things to sanctify, Islam clearly lays down the role of the mind in building the belief. This is also critical in discovering what is worshipped.

As for the manner by which humans worship the Creator, the mind has no role in it, nor can it know the Creator. This is because the organisation of the relationship of the human with the Creator cannot come from the created at all. Due to the mind not being able to comprehend the reality of the Creator it would be impossible for any human to organise their relationship with Him. Thus, it is impossible for anyone to design, organise and implement, by a limited mind, sanctification to the Creator. This is because such organisation requires comprehension of the reality of the Creator, a matter that is clearly impossible. Therefore, the system of worship must come from the Creator and not from the limited, dependent creation. Islam gives no role whatsoever to the human mind in defining the system of how to worship the creator.

It could be claimed that there is no need for humans to have a system of worship and that humans could perform acts of worship without a system at all. The problem with this is that the absence of their organisation would lead to anarchy, which would lead to incorrect or abnormal satisfaction. So if the procreational instinct required sexual satisfaction while it has no system for this satisfaction, then humans would try to satisfy it with anything that achieves it. This would lead it to abnormal satisfaction e.g. genital mutilation or incest. This also leads to deviation from the result of the satisfaction that is to procreate and give birth. The deviation would lead to a reduction in the production of offspring, if not stopping it altogether. This again leads to deviation of the instinct from the purpose it exists, which is the continuation of the human race.

Therefore, there must be a system that organises us. Islam established five basic forms of worship in order to sanctify the creator and satisfy the sanctification instinct. These are:

- The utterance of the testimony that there is no deity worthy of worship but Allah and that Muhammad (saw) is the Last and Final Messenger of Allah. This, in its entirety, is the basis of Islam.

- The establishment of *salaat* (prayer) by the individual and the community with all of its rules and prerequisites.

- The payment of Zakaat (alms), an annual financial obligation paid on specific wealth or capital they possess (rather than on earnings), exceeding a specific limit, to categories explained in the revelation. The specific details of which however are beyond the scope of this book.

- *Saum* (fasting) during the month of Ramadhan.

- The pilgrimage to Mecca (Hajj) once in a lifetime for those with the means to do so.

This is the manner in which Islam solves the problems of humans, which are derived from its sources.

In summary, the *Shari'ah* texts (the Qur'an and *ahadith*) are of detailed thought, the widest in scope for generalisation and the most fertile ground to cultivate general principles. In themselves they are suitable as legislative texts for different peoples and nations. This is because they cover all kinds of relationships, whether between individuals, the state and its citizens, or between states, peoples and nations. However new and multifarious these relationships may be, new thoughts can be deduced from the *Shari'ah* texts. Islam has the broadest scope for generalisation or interpretations, which can be seen from the grammar, sentences, words, style of expressions in terms of covering the wording (mantooq), meaning (mafhum), indication (*dalalah*) reasoning (ta'leel) and qiyas (analogy) based on the *Shari'ah* reason (*'Illah*) which makes deduction feasible, continuous and inclusive. This ensures the *Shari'ah* is able to encompass everything, issue or problem for all times and ages. As for being fertile ground for cultivating general principles, this is because of the abundance of general meanings contained within these texts. This is because the Qur'an and hadith were revealed in the form of broad guidelines even when focusing on specific details. The nature of these broad guidelines is that they give the Qur'an and hadith general meanings within which collective and detailed issues can be included and from this arise an abundance of general meanings. These general meanings contain real and perceptible issues and not hypothetical ones. At the same time they are revealed to solve the problems of all humanity, and not of specific individuals. As such, there exist over three hundred general principles (*qawa'id 'aammah*).

An example is the view on scientific and technological development. Islam like any other comprehensive ideological worldview has a view towards science as the *Shari'ah* texts came to deal with the matters humans face. Islam views technology, industry and material tools as a universal matter i.e. it is something which is common to all people and does not change according to the different beliefs, places or times. Islam views all tools, techniques and inventions as something that can be adopted because it is not a result of any foreign thought but rather just a result of progress. For this reason Islam not only permits the pursuit of science and technology but encourages it.

Islam views all the material matters which include the sciences, technology and industry, as merely the study of the reality and a study of how matter can be manipulated to improve the condition and living standards of humanity. This is the view of Islam on science and all its branches. The *Shari'ah* addressed this via numerous verses.

"It is He Who created for you all that is in the earth."   [TMQ Al-Baqarah:29]

, and

"Do you not see how Allah has made serviceable to you whatsoever is in the skies and whatsoever is in the earth, and He has loaded you with His favours, both the open and the hidden." [TMQ Luqman:20]

And,

"Who has appointed the earth a resting-place for you, and the sky a canopy; and caused water to pour down from the sky, thereby producing fruits as food for you." [TMQ Al-Baqarah:22]

And,

"And We send down from the sky blessed water whereby We give growth to gardens and the grain of crops. And lofty date palms with ranged clusters. Provision (made) for men…" [TMQ Qaf: 9-11]

These texts allow the general use of objects and materials that are found on or in the earth. From this is derived the Islamic *qaida* (principle):

"All objects are allowed unless *Shari'ah* evidence prohibits it".

Thus the initial view is that in generality all objects are permitted however their use has been restricted as all actions require a *Shari'ah* evidence. For instance Intercontinental Ballistic Missiles (ICBMs) are allowed in Islam.

However its use would require knowledge of the *Shari'ah* rule. ICBMs could be used for reasons ranging from legitimate deterrent measures to the illegitimate killing of innocent civilians. Islam permits the study and use of medicine, engineering, maths, astronomy, chemistry, physics, agriculture, industry, communications including the Internet, and the science of navigation and geography. This includes what results from them such as industry, tools, machinery and factories. Also included in this are industries, whether military or not, and heavy industry like tanks, aeroplanes, rockets, satellites, nuclear technology, hydrogen, electronic or chemical bombs, tractors, lorries, trains and steamships. This includes consumer industries and light weapons and the manufacture of laboratory instruments, medical instruments, agricultural tools, furniture, carpets and consumer products such as the TV, DVD and Playstation etc. The point being illustrated here is that all objects we know of past, present and future are allowed without restriction unless *Shari'ah* evidence exists to definitively disallow it.

Ijtihad proves **Islam's applicability**

The subject of *Ijtihad* occupies a recurring theme across much contemporary Islamic literature. *Ijtihad* is a tool employed by jurists, which keeps Islam relevant and applicable in the late-modern world. It is a genuine challenge for a book fourteen centuries old to deal with the rapid advances in technology and science as well as modern institutions.

Some have proposed reform (*islah*) as the tool for Islam's continual relevance, such schemes spring from viewing Islam through the prism of secular liberal democratic thought.

"*Ijtihad* is the Islamic tradition of critical thinking and independent reasoning. Now we have to re-discover it precisely to update Islam for the 21st century. The opportunity to update is especially available to Muslims in the West, because it's here that we enjoy precious freedoms to think, express, challenge and be challenged without fear of state reprisal. In that sense, the Islamic reformation has to begin in the West. I propose a non-military campaign to promote individual approaches to Islam, to re-discover our traditional critical thinking." *Irshad Manji, Interview by Dirk Verhofstadt, 'Muslims need critical thinking', Feb 2005, Institute for the Secularization of Islamic Societies.*

And,

"So it's not a Reformation or Enlightenment; in a sense we are engaging Islam in terms of its own dynamic, and the main dynamic here is the notion of *Ijtihad*, which means sustained reasoning. Now, *Ijtihad* is a crucial part of Islam, but the gates of *Ijtihad* were closed in the early part of the 13th, 14th century, by religious scholars – mainly for reasons of power, because they wanted to keep the interpretive power in their own hands. So what we are saying now it's time that we had new *Ijtihad*, that we had a new interpretation." *Islam in the modern world, Aug 2003, Zia Sardar, The Religion Report.*

The *Shari'ah* rules deal with human beings in their human context that is to say not in their regional or racial context. The *Shari'ah* deals exclusively with human nature which does not change with the passage of time.

Ijtihad is a legal tool employed by Islamic jurists to tackle contemporary problems using the existing *Shari'ah* sources. It is utilised to extract legislation where the *Shari'ah* has not already definitely addressed the matter at hand and is a defined process established and confirmed by the Messenger Muhammad (saw). It effectively allows the finite number of Islamic texts to address, in detail, previously unfamiliar events. The key component that makes this possible is the analogous process of linking the subject matter of the reality at hand to similar occurrences in the Islamic texts. *Ijtihad* consists of three stages:

1. Understanding the reality of the problem
2. To identify the Islamic texts which address a relevant or similar subject matter.
3. Identifying the similarities and differences between the current issue and the text and weighing these differences and similarities to extract a rule for the contemporary problem

Each of these elements is progressively more detailed requiring expertise and experience in Islamic jurisprudence, Islamic sources, Islamic legal maxims, the Arabic language (both pre- and post-revelation), legal definitions and more. *Ijtihad* is open to all that have the competency to do so. This process is by no means reserved for a priestly class or only one gender, rather what is required is the facility to comprehend and apply.

An example of an application of *Ijtihad* is on the current state of Muslim affairs. Numerous problems have befallen the Muslims including their lack of unity, their absence as an entity from the world arena, the chronic disorder, poverty and endemic corruption, their brutal, deceitful rulers and the fact their lands implement other than Islam. This is a completely new reality since Muslims governed their affairs by Islam continuously from the time of Muhammad (saw) to the abolition of the Khilafah in what is now known as Turkey on 3rd March, 1924 by Mustafa Kemal. Despite a veritable wealth of rulings on countless issues no Islamic ruling exists for what to do when the Khilafah is uprooted, the *Shari'ah* suspended and the Muslim community divided and directionless, defenceless and destitute. Muslim jurists never imagined such a tragic situation could ever arise and even if they did so they still would not have derived a rule for it as the principle is that a jurist must deal with reality as opposed to an imagined scenario.

In the current climate one could easily assume that Islam is unable to deal with such a new reality. Eminent policy makers, personalities and academics, both Muslim and non-Muslim, have taken turns for years constantly presenting their personal opinions on how the Muslims could reverse the situation often leaving us with more questions than answers. However it is abundantly clear the methodology required to revive the Muslims from their relentless decline will require the process of *Ijtihad* since we have already established that Islam is applicable for all times and instances and also that there is no existing *Shari'ah* rule.

Following the stages of *Ijtihad*, we look first to the reality. There is no Dar-ul Islam (land of Islam) today. Dar-ul Islam has been defined as a territory where the authority applies the *Shari'ah* absolutely and where the security of the state is maintained by the Muslims themselves both at home and abroad. There is only one situation in history where the Muslims were without Islamic authority and changed the situation to Dar-ul Islam. This was when

Muhammad (saw) worked to transform the corrupted societies by carrying Islam against the idol-worshippers in Mecca, galvanised public opinion for Islam in the peninsula, persistently sought military support from various tribes and later completely implemented Islam in Medina. *Ijtihad* in this case would be to examine the steps leading to the point of establishment and derive a method applicable today.

We could consider other issues that might affect humanity. One such example would be the use of military intelligence and spying. An example would be satellite technology to spy on the enemy; would this be something that the Muslims could utilise? Could the bugging of the control centres, computers and phones of the enemy be acceptable? Indeed we would find again that the Islamic texts are capable of dealing with such issues. If we study the Qur'an we would find that it is not allowed to spy on the citizens of the Islamic State, Muslim or not, since Allah (swt) mentioned in the Qur'an:

"And spy not on each other." (TMQ Al-Hujurat: 12)

This however does not apply to foreign enemies as Muhammad (saw) actively encouraged such activity. In these cases the jurists and scholars of Islam would look at the use of information warfare, bugging, spying and satellite technology from the angle of monitoring foreign belligerents.

The substantial progress made in early Islamic history, noted by many historians, owes much to the use of *Ijtihad*. It allowed the Khilafah to tackle many economic, political and social problems not previously confronted by Muhammad (SAW). The expansion of the Khilafah into new lands brought it into contact with foreign cultures, customs, languages, traditions and political structures. These included Greek, Persian, Roman, Berber, Asian and Assyrian. This created internal challenges of distribution and production of wealth, rights of minorities, administration of an expanding ruling apparatus, judiciary, appointment of local governors and accountability. These challenges provided a continuous demand for *Ijtihad* and resulted in the expansion of juristic writing, a rich legislative atmosphere, the development of madhahib (schools of thought) and with it the development of some of the most accomplished scholars in Islamic history.

It was not until after the ransacking of Baghdad by the Mongols in 1258 that the Khilafah felt that all contemporary incidents had already been catered for within the body of the richest legislative discourse ever seen by humanity. They reasoned prematurely that there was no longer a place for *Ijtihad*. Thus Muslims resorted to adopting the opinions of others rather than striving to derive their own or even to fully understand the juristic opinion presented. Allowing another to guide one to the Islamic ruling taqleed (imitation) and most people soon became muqali*deen* (imitators) to the existing schools of thought. The Islamic thought that had flourished and driven forward the Islamic civilisation soon stalled as creativity was ebbed away only to be replaced by intellectual apathy.

For a while these schools of thought remained content but this was put to an end with the emergence of a distinctly more ideological Europe in the seventeenth century. In the face of a massive intellectual challenge the repercussions of the abolishment of *Ijtihad* became apparent. The technological and intellectual challenges facing the Muslims required a response, which the Muslims were unable to provide from Islam since they had abandoned the process that would have given them access to Islam's rulings on new issues. No one doubted that Islam could deal with the issues presented but no one knew how to retrieve the answers.

With *Ijtihad* absent the Khilafah was unable to respond to these challenges and a bizarre scenario occurred where basic technology like the printing press, steam engines, electricity and telephones were outlawed but legislative codes from Europe were incorporated into Islamic governance and jurisprudence. This led to a number of individuals leading and championing Islamic reform such as Jamal ad-*Deen* al-Afghani (1839-1897), Sir Sayyid Ahmed Khan (1828-1898), Mohammed Abduh (1849–1905) and Taha Hussein (1889-1973). However, for Muslims at large reform offered no alternative but was rather an implicit attack on Islam's ability to deal with modern life. It also heralded a call to integrate into Europe's own intellectual and political culture.

Advocates of reform today still use the misguided train of thought of their 'modernist' predecessors. They call for the "revival of *Ijtihad*" in a purely secular context misunderstanding the term itself. This understanding can be refuted from understanding the very definition of *Ijtihad* which is derived from its linguistic understanding.

Ijtihad is derived from the Arabic root word 'j-h-d', which has connotations of struggle. From this root word jihad is derived – which is the struggle to make Allah's word the highest. Also from the same root *'mujahid'* is derived who is an individual that fights to make Allah's word the highest. *Ijtihad* is also derived from the same root which is the struggle or effort undertaken; in comprehending the most likely opinion about an issue from the *Shari'ah* rules in a manner that the Mujtahid feels unable to do any more.

Although *Ijtihad* stems from the Arabic root verb 'j-h-d', which has connotations of struggle, *Ijtihad* cannot be taken to mean unrestricted struggle. The *Shari'ah* definition is to struggle in a particular way defined as 'exerting the utmost effort in studying a problem thoroughly and deriving the most likely Islamic ruling on an indefinite issue via the process of referring strictly to Islamic sources up to the point of feeling unable to contribute anymore.'

In other words, it is the comprehension of the *Shari'ah* text from Qur'an and Sunnah after exerting one's upmost effort in arriving at this comprehension to gain understanding from amongst the most likely opinions. This means three issues need to be fulfilled in the derivation of the *Shari'ah* rule before it can be said the Mujtahid has performed a legitimate *Ijtihad*; and these are:

- Exerting effort in a manner until one feels unable to exert anymore;
- This exertion should be to find the most probable opinion about an issue from the *Shari'ah* rules amongst all the potential opinions.
- This opinion about an issue should be derived from the *Shari'ah* texts alone as they are the only sources from Allah (swt).

The *Shari'ah* is the speech of the Legislator relating to the actions of his servants. So the one who does not exert effort in reconciling evidences, understanding the circumstances of revelation and the chronology of the hadith, is not considered a Mujtahid. Also whoever exercises ones effort in seeking the most probable opinion regarding something other than the *Shari'ah* rules and information is not considered a Mujtahid either. Whoever seeks an opinion from the *Shari'ah* rules using other than the *Shari'ah* texts is not considered a Mujtahid. The Mujtahid is therefore restricted in making great effort in understanding the *Shari'ah* texts to deduce the Hukm of Allah (swt). The issue of *Ijtihad* is restricted to comprehension of the *Shari'ah* texts after exerting maximum effort for the sake of reaching this understanding to know the Hukm of Allah (swt). Thus the *Shari'ah* texts are the object of comprehension and they are the object of seeking the most probable opinion from the *Shari'ah* rules. Any reference to another source or a rule which brings benefit is not *Ijtihad*.

Modern reformers miss this point completely by narrowing *Ijtihad* to the linguistic meaning of 'juhd' (lit: exertion, effort or struggle) which for them was taken to mean to exert independent intellectual efforts. This amounted to limitless freethinking in whatever direction one wished as opposed to sincerely seeking the *Shari'ah* rule.

Islam is not a stranger to foreign ideas or alternative cultures. Numerous issues have arisen in recent times in the medical world as well as the industrial sector. All have been addressed by utilising the process of *Ijtihad*. *Ijtihad*, once placed in its correct context, is conclusive proof of the applicability of Islam for all times and instances.

Via the process of *Ijtihad* many contemporary issue have been addressed, for example:

In Vitro Vertalisation (IVF) was addressed by using the rules of kinship and the permissibility of seeking medical treatment.

Cloning was addressed by looking at the rules for the production of children, kinship and lineage

Life support machines were addressed by the general evidences for seeking treatment.

Advanced weaponry was addressed by the general permissibility of objects.

Genetically modified foods were addressed by using the evidences for the improvement of the quality of plants and food.

The Penicillin was addressed by the evidences which promote the finding of cures for disease

The double-helix structure of DNA again was addressed by the general evidences for seeking cures

Nuclear technology was addressed by the numerous evidences which indicate the preparing of deterrents and the general permissibility of objects, and

E-commerce was addressed by the evidences which permit the use of the non-civilisational matters.

Difference of opinion (*ikhtilaaf*) proves Islam's dynamism

Many academics have today studied Islam and in order to make it fit into the status quo and current world order cite the science of Ikhtilaaf to justify Capitalist concepts. The chief reason for this is that any revival is measured in the West against only one benchmark - Western secular liberalism. Anything conforming to this is progress and everything else is not. This is the Western view when revival is studied; therefore the secular environment is viewed as a universal one. The result of the process Europe underwent is known as civilisation and anything else is backward. This is the basis of the orientalist argument i.e. that we must rid ourselves of a medieval culture called Islam unless it can be reinterpreted or reformed. At the same time there has been an unfortunate tendency for some Muslims to misinterpret and even abuse some verses in response.

The fundamental reason why such numerous opinions can be derived from the Qur'an, one hundred and fourteen chapters in length, comprising only 6,236 verses is due to the fact that legitimate interpretations can be extrapolated i.e. one verse can be applied to more then one reality or that there can be a genuine iktilaaf (legitimate difference of opinion within certain, restricted boundaries). The primary reason for this is because most verses of the Qur'an are of a general nature which allows a wide spectrum of derivation. There can be different interpretations of some words and verses taking into account that some verses and their words are general, some specific, some implying restriction, whilst others have metaphorical and alluded meanings. This is what enables Islam to have diverse answers to the wide-ranging issues that may arise.

Difference of opinion is permitted in Islam and has always occurred. However, it is important we view this in an ideological context. This does not mean any individual can interpret the *Shari'ah* texts in whatever manner desired in order to conform to every whim or impulse. In Islam differences of opinion are permitted in areas where the Qur'an or *ahadith* allow such a process. The nature of the Arabic language is that one root word can have a number of derivatives therefore differences of interpretation can occur i.e. the reality of the word can be applicable upon numerous realities. There is however a restriction to this. Words in the Arabic language have two elements when anyone is looking to understand, interpret and apply. This is the mantooq (wording) and mafhoom (meaning). This means that interpretation cannot go beyond the meaning being indicated by the wordings. As an example the following verse could incorrectly and maliciously be used to justify homosexuality:

"O mankind! We have created you male and female, and have made you into nations and tribes in order that you may get to know one another"   [TMQ Al Hujaraat:13]

This verse is general as its an address to mankind, so it would encompass both Muslim, non-Muslim, male and female and *'get to know each other'* could be interpreted as including sexual relationships between the same genders. However this understanding cannot be extrapolated from the wording of this verse as this contradicts numerous other verses:

"We sent Lut when he said to his people: What! do you commit an indecency (lewdness) such that no one in the world has not done before you? For you practice your lusts on men over women. You are an extravagant people"   [TMQ 7:80]

, and

"What! Of all the creatures of the world will you approach males and leave what your Lord has created for you of your wives? You are a people exceeding limits"

[TMQ 26:165]

Hence interpretation has rules and restrictions and is not a limitless process where one can interpret however they wish. Another example is that of interest (Riba), it has been argued that the lender bears the risk of lending money therefore the interest he receives is due compensation for this. It has also been argued that the Islamic texts need to be interpreted in a way which does allow interest as the value of money decreases over time and the lender should receive interest to cover this loss in value. Some have even argued that Islam only forbade high interest as this was the common form at the time the verses of Qur'an were revealed:

"And Allah has permitted trade and forbidden Interest"   [TMQ al Baraqa:275]

The term Riba (interest) as found in the above verse and in other verses of the Qur'an and Hadith came in a general form. This includes every form of interest because it is a generic name associated with the letters alif and lam (the) - meaning that all forms of usury are included whatever its type, whether it is a Riba that was well known at the time of the Messenger of Allah (saw) or a Riba that is not known and therefore a new issue. Therefore, there can be no place for making Halaal any form of Riba, because the prohibition has come in a general form. The general term will remain general unless there is evidence that restricts or specifies the term i.e. another evidence would need to be sought. In this case there is no evidence to specify it, so Riba can only be considered in its general meaning. Texts which are not of a conclusive nature can be extrapolated to whatever is possible by the limits of the wording and its meaning, on the condition that it does not contradict another evidence.

In every ideology there exists difference of opinion on solutions built upon the creedal tenets. Differences however are never in the creed but rather in the solutions that are derived from the creed. In democratic countries, numerous schools of thought have arisen due to differences in interpretation. In the US today we have Democrats and Republicans. In the UK we have Labour, Liberal Democrats and Conservatives. Across the Western world we have neo-conservatives as well as Libertarians, Fabians, Environmentalists and Christian Democrats. All differ in the manner that liberal ideas should manifest themselves but they all have secularism – the Capitalist creed - as their basis.

Economics is also prone to such difference with the Keynesian school, advocating government intervention, against the Monetarists. Socialism also had a number of schools of thought built upon their creed. Advocates of socialism saw the injustice that resulted from the concept of 'Freedom of Ownership' and concluded that the difference in private ownership between people was the problem that required a solution. One school of thought (the Communist school) advocated practical equality in everything and absolute abolition of private property. Another school of thought (the agrarian socialists) proposed abolishing private property in agricultural land only. Then came a third socialist school of thought (known as state socialism) where private property was transferred to public ownership in the name of public interest i.e. nationalization in every situation where public interest called for it.

Hence interpretation forms a key aspect of the implementation of an ideology; such work is carried out by jurists as well as judges. When the classical scholars laid down the rules for usool al *fiqh* (foundations of jurisprudence), established their schools of thought each jurist established various principals to ensure interpretation never deviated from the Islamic sources. These techniques ensured an interpretation remained within the boundaries of the wording and meaning being indicated. The Jurists incorporated into their schools of thought the fact that although understanding the root word is important, it is not enough in itself to understand words. The Arabic language existed before the revelation of the

Qur'an and all words already had their defined meanings and definitions. As a result a large section of Islamic jurisprudence is dedicated to the linguistic and Shari' meanings of Arabic words. An example of this would be the word taubah. Linguistically it means 'turning' but the *Shari'ah* definition is repentance. The root word alone therefore is not enough to understand or interpret taubah. However understanding the root word is still important. This can be illustrated when Islamic jurists tell us the *Shari'ah* definition of repentance requires us to 'turn' away from forbidden thoughts, desires and deeds and 'turn' back to Allah (swt).

The cause of revelation is also an indicator to how each verse of Qur'an can be understood and applied however rulings are taken from the generality of the text and not from the specificity of the cause. This contributes to verses extending to differing realities otherwise each verse would be irretrievably linked to a specific situation that may never arise again. The fact that this principle exists is healthy and actually ensures Islamic jurisprudence is enriched with answers to contemporary incidents. However this principal also clearly shows a jurist the boundaries to interpretation.

In summary the process of interpretation or understanding texts is a very precise science. Like any process it is regulated by strict protocols and procedures. This is akin to conducting a scientific experiment; it would require knowledge of materials, methods, formulae and equations.

Applicability and adaptability (expansion)

The difference of opinion stems from the applicability of a legislative principle or verse upon numerous incidents. In Islam this is possible, as many of the rules have come within a general scope thus many rulings can be deduced from it. Islam is expansive enough to respond to all the new events. However many of these events may arise over the course of time. Below are a selection of rulings, outlining how they are derived from the Islamic sources, how they are applicable upon multiple realities and how the expansion in Islamic jurisprudence makes Islam relevant for all times and ages.

Inheritance

"Concerning (the inheritance) for your children: to the male is the equivalent of the portion of two females, and if they (children) were women more than two, then theirs is two-thirds of the inheritance."　　　　　　　　　　　　　　　　　　(TMQ An-Nisa: 11)

1. We understand that the male child takes double that which the female child takes.

2. We also understand that the child of the son (grandchild) is treated as the child in cases where there are no living children, because the grandchild is included in the word *'Walad'* 'children.'

3. This is contrary to the children of the daughter, who are not treated like the children of the son where there are no living children. This is so because the children of the daughter are not included linguistically in the Arabic word for children *'Walad'*

4. We understand also that if the children were females, and more than two in number, then they share in two-thirds of the inheritance. The Prophet (saw) made for the two females a portion equivalent to those who are more than two. So the rule in regard to the two females is the same rule for more than two females.

Intellectual property

"And give them from the property of Allah, which He gave to you."

(TMQ An-Nur: 33)

"And spend from what He put you in charge of."   (TMQ Hadid: 7)

"And He has provided you with properties and offspring."   (TMQ Nuh: 12)

"O you who believe Spend of the good things which you have earned, and of that which we bring forth from the earth for you."   (TMQ Al-Baqarah: 267)

1. We understand from these verses that ownership in Islam is the permission of the Legislator for one to benefit from an asset. Private ownership is determined by the *Shari'ah* rule; this ascribes an asset or a service to an individual, thus enabling one to benefit from the asset and service itself. Thus, the right to own a thing does not arise from the thing itself or from the fact that it is beneficial as in the Capitalist model.

2. We also understand that ownership in Islam includes the right of disposal. The individual has authority over the thing that he owns. Islam enabled him to freely dispose of it and benefit from what he owns according to the *Shari'ah* rules. It also obliged the Khilafah to protect private ownership and laid down punishments to deter those who infringe upon the ownership of others.

3. We also understand that thoughts are not subject to ownership. However all ideas originate from the mind, hence the mind is the initial 'home' for any particular thought from the perspective of reality. Thus one can ignore it or dispense of it seeking a material value. However, once dispensed it cannot be copyrighted or patented as ownership has been transferred and the new owner has full rights of disposal.

4. On the other hand trademarks are sensed, tangible and have a material value because it is a component of trade. Therefore, it is allowed for an individual to own it and the Khilafah is obliged to protect this right of the individual who will be able to freely dispose of it, and others will be prevented from infringing upon this right.

5. We also deduce the definition of ownership which is the 'permission of the legislator to benefit from an asset or service.'

Nanotechnology

Nanotechnology, is the development and production of artefacts in which a dimension of less than 100 nanometres (nm) is critical to functioning (1 nm = 10-9 m/40 billionths of an inch) (atom 0.1 nm, DNA (width) 2nm, Protein 5 - 50nm, virus 75-100nm, bacteria 1,000 -10,000nm, white blood cells 10,000nm) Nanotechnology holds out the promise of materials of precisely specified composition and properties, which could yield structures of unprecedented strength and computers of extraordinary compactness and power. Nanotechnology may lead to revolutionary methods of atom-by-atom manufacturing and to surgery on the cellular scale.

The Islamic ruling on all objects is that in origin they are all permissible. The study, research and development of such objects is permitted and allowed for all Muslims to undertake. Its use and the manner in which it can be deployed is restricted, therefore the uses of Nanotechnology would require an evidence for it to be used in a specific manner. It would not be permissible to use Nanotechnology to create objects and material where the domestic population could be spied upon as this is something Islam condemned. However Islam has made it obligatory for the Khilafah to have industry in order for machines and heavy industrial goods to be produced. This is for defence purposes. For this endeavour the Khilafah can produce all the latest weaponry (conventional, biological, nuclear or chemical) for deterrent purposes. It is not allowed to wipe out the enemy by using Nanotechnology as well as by any other technology.

In summary, Nanotechnology is perfectly permissible in many areas including, but not specific to, the areas of medicine and biology as well as optics and aeronautics.

Stem Cells

"Do not kill yourselves."   [TMQ An-Nisa: 29]

The Messenger of Allah (saw) said: "Get married to the tender and fertile (women) for indeed I will vie in your great numbers."

[Reported by Abu Dawud].

Qatada narrated from al-Hasan who narrated from Samurah that he (saw) said "The Prophet (saw) forbade us from celibacy" (reported by Ahmad)

1. From the above evidences we can deduce that stem cells derived from early embryos, which are no longer needed for infertility treatment ('spare embryos') from the *Shari'ah* point of view is allowed.

2. IVF, as a means to aid fertilization between a husband and wife, is allowed according to the numerous evidences (including the above) that recommend Muslims to marry and reproduce.

The nature of the IVF process is that embryos will be formed that will not be needed for placement in the woman's womb. These can be utilized for the purpose of producing stem cells.

3. We also understand that the use of adult tissues to produce stem cells is allowed if a living person gave their consent. This is because the person has a legal authority over their organs in Islam. From the *Shari'ah* point of view each individual has the final say over their organs during their lives and has the right to make decisions regarding them. Hence, one can donate his organ to somebody else who needs it. However, for a donor to donate an organ the organ should not be vital for his own life. This is derived from the ayah in sur'ah an-Nisa.

4. Not only does Islam allow stem cell research, but it could potentially throw the field wide open. The present model of using supernumerary embryos has met with limited success in producing embryonic stem cell lines. Present research, though not conclusive, is suggesting that higher quality embryos such as blastocysts lead to a higher efficiency of embryonic stem cell production (Cowan et al, 2004). Blastocysts are the collection of cells that are in the next developmental stage from the embryo. From an Islamic jurisprudential perspective it is acceptable to use foeti up to the age of 42 days for stem cell extraction and hence the potential exists for the highly refined production of stem cells. Islam has laid down clear boundaries to demarcate what is allowed and what is not via the *Shari'ah*. Stem cells can be used from live adults, umbilical cords, IVF embryos and aborted foeti under 42 days gestation. They cannot be extracted through human cloning, dead human tissue and foeti above 42 days.

Cloning

"And that He (Allah) created the pairs, male and female. From Nutfah (drops of semen – male and female discharges) when it is emitted."   (TMQ An-Najm:45-46)

"Was he not a Nutfah (drops of semen) poured forth? Then he became a clot; then (Allah) shaped and fashioned (him) in due proportion. And made him in two sexes, male and female."   (TMQ Al-Qiyamah:37-39)

The Messenger of Allah (saw) said: "For every disease Allah created its cure" (Bukhari)

1. From these evidences we understand that the production of children via cloning is different from the natural way that Allah (swt) has made humans to reproduce their offspring.

2. We also understand that the children who are born out of cloning females, without a male, have no fathers. In addition, they will not have mothers if the egg that was merged with the nucleus of the cell was placed in the womb of a female different from that female whose egg was used in the cloning process. This is the case because the female whose womb was used to implant the egg is no more than a place to house the egg. This will lead to the loss of that human, where he has no father and no mother.

3. We also understand that their will be a loss of kinship. Islam has obligated preserving affinity and maintaining it. The cloning which aims at producing people who are outstanding in terms of their intelligence, strength, health, and beauty would mean choosing the people with characteristics among the males and the females regardless of if they were married couples or not. As a result, the cells would be taken from the males who had the required characteristics, and the eggs would be taken from selected women and

implanted in selected women. This would lead to the kinship being lost and mixed.

4. The production of children through cloning prevents applying many of the *Shari'ah* rules, such as the rules of marriage, kinship, alimony, fatherhood, inheritance, custody, *maharim* (people forbidden for marriage due to blood relationship e.g. mother, sister etc.) in addition to many other *Shari'ah* rules. The affinity would get mixed and would be lost. This goes against the natural way that Islam views reproduction.

5. We also understand that cloning plants and animals can improve quality and increase productivity and aid in finding cures for many common human diseases. The improvement in the quality of plants and animals and the increase of productivity is not prohibited from a *Shari'ah* perspective, and it is among the things that are allowed. Also, the use of plants and animal cloning to cure human diseases, especially acute ones, is allowed in Islam. It is even recommended because seeking a cure for illness is recommended and manufacturing medicine for curing is recommended. Therefore, it is allowed to use the cloning process to improve the quality of plants and to increase their productivity. It is also allowed to use the cloning process to improve the quality of cows, sheep, camels, horses, and other animals, in order to increase productivity of these animals and to increase their numbers, and to utilise this to cure many of the human diseases especially the acute ones. Thus cloning plants and animals is permitted from Islam.

6. Foetal cloning is where the zygote is formed in the womb of a wife as a result of the husband's sperm and the wife's egg. That zygote is divided into many cells, which can divide and grow. These cells are divided so that each cell becomes a foetus by itself, as a duplicate of the original zygote. If one or more of these zygotes were implanted in the wife's womb (who was the source of the original cell) then this form of cloning is permitted because it

is the multiplying of the zygote, which existed in the wife's womb through a medical procedure to bring about identical twins. However apart from this we understand human cloning is not permitted in Islam.

Public properties

The Messenger of Allah (saw) said:

"Muslims are partners (associates) in three things: in water, pastures and fire"   [Narrated by Ibn 'Abbas and reported by Abu Dawud].

The Messenger of Allah (saw) said:

"Three things are not prevented from (the people); the water, the pastures and the fire"   [Ibn Majah narrated from Abu Hurairah]

"Abyadh ibn Hammal came to the Prophet (saw) and asked him to grant him a salt laden land and he granted it to him. And when he left, one person in attendance with the Prophet (saw) said, "Do you know what you granted him? You granted him the uncountable water (Al-'udd)". He (saw) then took it away from him."   [Narrated from At-Tirmidhi]

1. We deduce a number of rulings from these three Hadiths and generate a collective principal. This is achieved by combining a number of rulings or deriving a rule from a general verse.

2. We understand that public property is the permission of the Lawgiver to the community to share the use of an asset. Assets which are public property are those which the Lawgiver stated as belonging to the community as a

whole, and those which individuals are prevented from possessing as indicated by the first two hadith.

3. These evidences show that people are partners and associates in water, pastures and fire, and that the individual is prohibited from possessing them. In origin no reason is given to why utilities are public properties and implies that these three things are the only ones which represent public property with no consideration given to their depiction for the community's need for them.

4. However, there were occasions when the Prophet (saw) allowed such public property to be owned by individuals. It is known that the Prophet (saw) allowed water in At-Taif and Khaybar to be owned by individuals, and it was used for irrigating their plants and farms. Had the sharing of water been just because it is water and not because of the consideration of the community's need for it, then he would not have allowed individuals to possess it. So from his permission to individuals to possess the water, it can be deduced that the *Illah* (reasonn) of partnership in the water, pastures and fire, is their being of the community utilities that are indispensable to the community. Hence anything that qualifies as being indispensable to the community is a community utility, which is considered a public property, whether or not it was water, pasture or fire i.e. whether it was specifically mentioned in the Hadith or not

5. We also understand that the minerals found in the Earth of uncountable quantity which cannot be normally depleted are also considered a public property and should not be possessed individually due to the hadith from Tirmidhi.

6. We understand that when he (saw) realised that the salt mine was of a large quantity he reversed his grant and took it back thereby prohibiting its

ownership by individuals. Thus it was not the salt, but rather the salt mine who's ownership was prohibited individually as when Muhammad (saw) came to know it was non-depletable he prohibited its private ownership, despite the fact that he knew it was salt and that he had initially granted it.

7. This rule, that the uncountable and un-depleted minerals are considered a public property, includes all minerals, whether they on the surface of the earth such as salt, coal, sapphire, ruby, and the like. As well as gold, silver, iron, copper, lead and the like. This includes whether they are solid like crystal, or fluid like oil. All of them are minerals, which are included within the meaning of the Hadith.

8. We also understand that there are some items whose nature prevents them from coming under the domain of individual ownership. They are different to the public properties in the sense that in origin they cannot be individually owned. So Water, for example, could be possessed by individuals, but this is prohibited if the community cannot manage to live without it, unlike the case with roads which certainly cannot be owned by any individual. Therefore, although the evidence for this category is that the reason (*Illah*) is applicable to it and that it is from the community utilities, however its nature indicates that it belongs to the public property. This category includes roads, rivers, seas, lakes, public canals, gulfs, straits, dams and the like.

9. Thus the principal "The people are partners in the water, pastures and fire" was derived from a set of evidences and can be used to define the various properties within the Khilafah and can be used and applied instead of finding the individual evidences whenever an issue of ownership over items arises

Commerce

"Then if they give suckle to your children, give them their due payment ..."

[TMQ 65:6]

The Messenger of Allah (saw) said: "Give the worker his wage before his sweat dries."

Al-Bara'a bin 'Aazib and Zayd bin Arqam were (two) partners, so they bought silver with cash and on credit. This news reached the Messenger of Allah (saw) and he said to them

"that (part) which was in cash, allow it, and that (part) which was in credit, return it back."

Muhammed (saw) narrated that: Allah said "I am the third of the two partners as long as neither of them betrayed his companion. If one of them betrayed the other then I would come out from them."

The Prophet (saw) also said: "the profit is according to the conditions placed by the contractors, and the loss is according to the amount of the property or fund."

1. From these hadiths and ayah we can deduce the conditions for contracts in Islam which is the offer and acceptance of a permissible thing or service. We also understand that Islam made a contract between two people and not by the actions of one person.

2. We can also deduce the permissibility of employment, which is likened to hiring. Hence the skill of the engineer, doctor and technician is hired. We

also deduce one of the conditions for employment is the agreement over the wage.

3. We can also deduce the permissibility of leasing and representation as these are just extensions of hiring.

4. We can also deduce the definition of a company and its conditions. The *Sharika* (Company) is an agreement between two or more people to do some type of work in order to make profit.

5. We understand from these evidences that one of the conditions for a valid company in Islam is that the debts of the company are distributed in proportion to the capital between the partners i.e. there is no limited liability.

6. We can also deduce the different types of company structures from the above evidences:

The company of equals (al-'inan) this is where both partners put their money into a business and work with it. Both partners would have the right to buy and sell and take the company forward, hence all partners are all equal in their deposal.

The company of bodies (al-abdan) this is where two or more people come together with their skills such as a consultant, doctor or craftsmen. Although they use their money, the skill they have is what constitutes the basis of the company.

The company of body and capital (mudharaba) this is where one funds the capital of the business and the other partner works with it. The partner who provides the capital element is a silent partner and takes no part in the running of the business. The other partner buys and sells on behalf of the company.

The company of reputation (*wujooh*) this is a company similar to madharabah but the capital is provided by a silent partner who has respect and standing and based upon this the company trades. The partner could be a rich merchant, which would mean debts will always be paid by this company as they are backed by a wealthy individual. Company of Negotiation (Mufawadha) this is any combination of the above.

Conclusion

The call for an Islamic reformation is being fought using an array of styles and means and various political actions are being undertaken ensuring the ummah itself changes Islam, with this in mind the following points need to be understood when defending Islam:

1. Various surveys, think-tank reports and policy makers have all accepted that Muslims globally have rejected Western values. This represents a glaring failure on the part of the West as it has faced no challenges to its global supremacy. This means the battle for hearts and minds and physical occupation represents a last ditch effort to salvage the emergence of an alternative system of governance. Thus defending Islam should be undertaken from the perspective of a position of strength rather than a position of weakness.

2. The call for reformation and subverting foreign thoughts has historically been the approach Capitalism undertook to defend itself from challenges to its supremacy. The Cold War is the best example of this; the defence of the ideology included the McCarthyism purges as well as anti-communist propaganda. Europe today defends itself by concocting lies (subverting) all those who oppose 'European values' or 'National values' as dangerous, extremist, radical, fundamentalist, a potential terrorist and a national security threat. As a result it is seen as perfectly legitimate for the state police to monitor Muslims by bugging their phones, monitoring their histories, tracking their movements abroad and arresting them with mere suspicion even though they have not actually committed a crime, but just hold certain views which are different to those held in wider society. The point here being these actions are being undertaken to defend Capitalism from a potential rival.

3. This is not the first attempt undertaken to reform Islam, in 1857 the British East India Company faced uprisings in India which mobilised the masses and threatened to end British rule in India. Jihad had been officially declared on the British by the Ulema of hind and faced with the prospect of defeat attempts to pacify Muslim opposition lead the British Empire to turn to Mirza Gulam Ahmed who was leader of a small group of people who denied jihad. Gulam said: *"Behold! I have come to you people with a directive that henceforth jihad with the sword has come to an end but jihad for the purification of your souls still remains. This injunction is not from me but rather it is the will of God."*[24] He forbade fighting the Empire due to his favor for British rule and support, in a letter to Queen Victoria he said *'…For the sake of the British government, I have published fifty thousand books, magazines and posters and distributed them in this and other Islamic countries. It is as the result of my endeavours that thousands of people have given up thoughts of Jihad which had been propounded by ill-witted mullahs and embedded in the minds of the people. I can rightly feel proud of this that no other Muslim in British India can equal me in this respect…'*[25] This attempt lead to the British inventing a new faith and creating a new 'prophet', such a vain attempt gained no currency with the Muslim masses, instead hardening opposition to British colonialism.

4. Any attack on the Islamic ideology, *Shari'ah* rules or identity needs to be understood in this context. Thus all attempts at explaining Islam require adherence to the Islamic rules whatever the pressure as the plan to reform Islam is a plan for Muslims themselves to reform Islam. Any twisting of the *Shari'ah* rules or defence of Islam incorrectly will result in aiding the West and treachery from the perspective of Islam. Any explanation of a *Shari'ah* rule should take the approach of explaining the rule, outlining the principal it is built upon and the source it is derived from. This approach shows clearly the ideological linkage between the solution/rule and the creed and ensures those who are smitten by reform will be unable to twist Islam.

5. Apostasy should be discussed by explaining that what is being discussed is an alternative ideology, an alternative conception of life and an alternative way of organising life's affairs to the current secular model. There exist some fundamental differences between the two models - the secular and Islamic models are not the same. They do not overlap as they do not stem from the same fundamental ideas. They will therefore have entirely different impressions of how society should look.

Since secularism and Islam do not agree at the basis it is wholly inappropriate to judge this alternative using the secular model as a benchmark. Doing so would inevitably lead to the elimination of any methodology not in agreement with secularism before the discourse even commenced - No debate on secularism would ever take place! If Islam is an alternative way to organise life it will inevitably have solutions which are the complete opposite to the secular model.

Non - agreement with the secular basis is not proof in itself to render an idea invalid. Would we consider the Cuban healthcare system wrong because it is not built upon the free market model, even though it's the best healthcare system in the world which the Cuban state subsidizes?

Entering into Islam is essentially entering a contract. There can be no compulsion in it. People enter into Islam based on free will. As there is no force the intellectual conviction must be overwhelming especially since someone entering into Islam willingly knows full well there can be no return to non-Islam due to the death penalty - This cements the need for intellectual conviction. It also prevents those who would seek to publicly become Muslim then publicly apostate in order to bring doubt in the ideology. No ideological state would allow its basis to be openly questioned in society as this would lead to the weakening and possible removal and replacement of the ideology by another.

Apostasy is a question of what kind of person would openly and publicly abandon Islam with full knowledge that they will be killed for it, rather than either keeping it to themselves or leave the Khilafah. Hence, the death penalty only applies on those who in the Khilafah openly leave Islam, and choose to remain in the state despite knowing the law; this is considered an open attack on the basis of the state which is Islam, essentially it is viewed as treason and a political attack on the Khilafah in order to undermine it. No ideology would tolerate this. It is understood from surveying the Islamic evidences, the actions of Muhammad (saw) and the actions of the generations after him (the sahabah) those who chose to leave the fold of Islam require vigorous debate and discussion, where rational proofs are presented in the best way for a maximum of three days.

Thus the issue of apostasy forms part of the rules to do with the defence of the ideology. It can be seen that both capitalism and communism had mechanisms in place to protect their respective ideologies and they dealt very harshly with anyone among their citizens working to undermine them. It is in this context the Islamic rules of apostasy need to be understood. It also needs to be understood that Islam is not just a punishment system but has an economic system, social system as well as a ruling system. Our history shows when all of Islam was applied the Muslim world prospered and become the leading nation in the world.

6. The claim that Islam oppresses women and does not provide equality for them is a discussion about the Islamic evidences which treat the relations between the sexes and not one of Islam and equality. From the Islamic evidences we understand Islam does not value an action, a duty or an individual on the basis of how much they can contribute to the economy or the state. It values an individual, male or female, based upon whether their actions conform to the command of the Creator and their level of taqwa.

We see that the man and the woman share similar qualities in their nature, the obligation prescribed to both is the same such as the prayer, fasting, and Hajj. However, where the nature differs then different duties have been prescribed. So, the husband or father has been obligated with the responsibility of protecting the family and providing for them financially. The woman has been obligated with the primary role of ensuring the welfare of the family by nurturing the children and conveying the culture to them. Besides these she can pursue a career, engage in sports activities and run a business within the remit the *Shari'ah* has demanded of modesty.

Islam came with the *Shari'ah* commandments which it obliged on the man and the woman. When it clarified the *Shari'ah* rules which treat the actions of each of them, it did not give the issue of equality any attention. Rather it viewed that there was a problem that required a solution. So, it treated the actions regardless of whether it was a problem pertaining to a man or a woman. Thus, the solution was for the action of a human, for the incident, and not for the man or woman. Therefore, the question of equality or the lack of equality between the man and woman is not the subject of discussion. This expression is not present in Islamic legislation.

Rather what exists is the *Shari'ah* rule of an incident, which has resulted from a certain human whether it is from a man or a woman.

When the rights and obligations are for humans, one will find equivalence in these rights and obligations for both men and women. Thus, the rights and obligations will be for all, and assigned to all men and women as one, without difference or disparity. Hence, you will find that Islam did not differentiate between men and women when it invited people to Islam. Nor did it differentiate between men and women in the commandment of carrying the da'wah. It made the commandments relating to Islam such as worship, morals, Hajj, politics, employment and Zakaat the same in terms of their legal obligation.

When rights, obligations and commandments relate to the nature of a man or woman, in their physical, anatomical, biological and psychological make-up then their rights and obligations will be disparate due to their inherent differences. This is because the solutions are required for problems that arise from this inherent difference. The solution is therefore not for humans in general but to one gender in particular who possesses different characteristics from the other. When a problem is faced by one gender due to their specific nature or attribute, then the rule pertaining to that gender cannot be applied generally to everyone because only one gender faces the problem. Thus the general rules would not apply and specific rules that address the characteristic in question are required. An example of this is that Islam has ordered the attire of women be different from men, just as it has ordered that the attire of men should be different from the attire of women.

Equality is not the basis of Islam and never has been in the history of Islamic jurisprudence. This is a term alien to Islam. Many thinkers when they study the rules that Islam lays down for women do so from the angle of equality. Hence they look at inheritance, polygamy, clothing and the Islamic view on the public life from the view of equality. Thus polygamy should only be allowed if women can have the equivalent multiple marriages. Similarly with inheritance the claim is made that it should be equal from a monetary angle. The problem with such a mentality is that everything would be wrong, invalid and outdated as it doesn't agree with equality. So in a society where the women outnumber men polygamy would be considered invalid as it's not done equally even though it clearly solves the problem. The women's dress would be seen as oppressive because it's not the same as the male dress even if this creates a stable and unifying society.

Any study of any thought from the viewpoint of another ideology would be deeply flawed, biased and deficient from the outset. Therefore the discussion can never be about whether Islam complements, agrees or disagrees with liberal democracy, this implicitly makes one's belief the benchmark which is wrong. Making equality the universal benchmark brings up a whole host of other problems. Equality assumes sameness between the genders and would thus fall into trouble when faced with problems, which are gender specific.

7. Islam's view on homosexuality is another concept many have attacked. Many Muslims in endeavouring to defend Islam, eventually twist Islam in order to make it palatable. In regards to homosexuality a number of points need to be understood:

The social system in Islam came to regulate the relationships between men and women. It organised the satisfaction of the procreational instinct in a manner ensuring the reason for its creation is met.

From reality one can see that the procreation instinct can be satisfied in many ways; a man with a women, a man with a man, a women with a women and so on. However, such attempts at satisfaction will not serve the purpose of civilisational continuance for which the instinct has been created in humanity except in one case that is if a man satisfies it with a woman and a woman satisfies it with a man.

So the relationship of a man with a woman from the angle of instinctual sexuality is a natural relationship free from any abnormality in the eyes of Islam. It is the only relationship by which the survival of the human race is maintained. Thus all the Islamic rules in regards this instinct are oriented towards the survival of the species without distinction between men or women. Islam views the pleasure and enjoyment that is obtained by such satisfaction a natural and inevitable matter whether humanity considers it or not. This is the way Islam views the instinct and it laid down rules for both men and women upon this basis.

The Qur'an confirmed that the basis of the procreational instinct is the preservation of the human race. The result of this is that Islam restricted sexual relations between the male and females in marriage only.

"It is He who has created you from a single person, and He has created from him his wife, in order that he might enjoy the pleasure of living with her. When he had sexual relations with her, she became pregnant and she carried it about lightly. Then when it became heavy, they both invoked Allah, their Lord: If You give us a good child, indeed we shall be amongst the grateful." (TMQ Al- Araf: 189)

Any relations outside of this are considered a crime and have a punishment prescribed. The other kinds of relations which are external manifestations of the procreation instinct, such as parenthood, childhood, brotherhood, uncle hood, are allowed and considered of the unmarriageable kinship.

The legalisation of Homosexuality in the Western world is based upon a completely different depiction of life. This is inevitable as it has a different view on such an issue because its basis is different to Islam. Throughout the last 40 years the Western world legalised homosexuality due to the existence of consent and the state not interfering with the private lives of individuals, i.e. individual freedom of actions are matters of private morality.

How male-female relations should be regulated, which gender should have leadership, who should have the right of custody in the case of divorce is not a discussion upon the reality i.e. understanding the reality at hand does not lead one to a conclusion. What would be considered a valid relationship and what type of creature of whichever gender one should sleep with can never be a taken from the reality as the reality does not explain this. A man or women when stripped down to their organic needs or atomic or biological structure do not manifest themselves with answers of who they have relations with or who they should sleep with.

Neither is there any evidence from looking purely at men and women that show us how relations between them should be regulated. Therefore the answer must emanate from some point external to the reality i.e. a belief system or ideology.

It needs to be understood also that the empirical research attempted to justify homosexuality is highly disputed by the West itself and is largely speculative. Attempts at linking such behavior to the biological make-up of humans rests on research conducted on fruit flies. Research into the influence of hormones on sexual orientation rests on tests carried out on animals. Research into innate sexuality has long been exposed as the experiments were carried out on sex offenders.

Hence the discussion of homosexuality is a discussion of how the Islamic ideology regulates relations between people relative to capitalism. So it is liberals who need to prove the validity of homosexuality. The fact that the West believes in sexual freedoms does not prove its validity, it merely proves how such a thought was derived.

8. It needs also to be understood that the West started the battle to reform Islam and is pushing and forcing Muslims to change Islam. This is being achieved by blaming Islam for the existence of terrorism and by directly attacking some of the thoughts of Islam. The aim here is to push Muslims into twisting Islam under this pressure. Hence any defence of Islam needs to be undertaken with knowledge and without appeasement. One should bear in mind the example of the sahabah who were mocked when

Muhammad (saw) told the people of Mecca he went to the heavens on the night of Al Isra and Miraj. The sahabah didn't engage in appeasement or twist Islam to make it palatable to the people Mecca. Some sahabah explained if Muhammad (saw) has said so then it is true whilst some sahabah answered by going on the offensive and questioning the people of Mecca that have they ever known Muhammad (saw) to have lied. It is the duty of every Muslim to defend Islam hence every Muslim should acquaint themselves with the arguments against Islam and ensure they know the Islamic stance on such an issue. However the duty upon every Muslim is also to defend Islam correctly, this is only achieved by explaining the Islamic rule from the Islamic sources. Any other response is not explaining Islam, and is a disservice to Islam and has aided the reforming of Islam. It is narrated in a hadith that Muhammad (saw) said:

"there will come a time when holding onto Islam will be like holding scorching hot embers."

9. The issue of defending Islam correctly cannot be stressed enough. The ramifications of which if not done correctly will result in the removal of Islam as we know it. An example to illustrate this is what happened in the history of Islam with the expansion of the Khilafah. When the Muslims conquered the areas of al-sham (modern day Palestine, Lebanon and Syria) and Iraq Muslims came into contact with the Nestorian Christians who were well acquainted with the Philosophy of the ancient Greeks. The existence of ideas in any society would create a clash which inevitably creates an atmosphere of debate and discussion. This is exactly what happened when the early Muslims conquered lands. In al-Sham the Nestorian Christians used Greek philosophy to counter the dawah of the Muslims. All the Muslims who defended Islam did so with the only intention of furthering the dawah and cementing Islam in those lands. However the way one defends Islam is different to one's sincerity. Some Muslims responded by

attempting to use the ideas of Plato and Aristotle in the hope of convincing the Christians of Islam and at the same time refuting Greek philosophy. These Muslims used logic to achieve this and the Christians were using the same method. However problems occurred because such Muslims were not acquainted with such a process of thinking and in fact reached conclusions which contradicted the Islamic aqeedah.

Hence Greek ideas which seemingly agreed with Islam were considered valid and those that were not such as the discussion about fate and destiny, the mind, thought, the soul, the eternity of the speech of god and god's attributes were reconciled with Islam using logic. Such Muslims embraced the ancient's views taking Islam into account, hence reconciling Greek philosophy became the basis of the debate rather then the Islamic view on such issues. Such discussions and confusion occupied Muslims for centuries, led to the creation of sects based upon ideas which contradicted Islam and some such as the Mut'azilah turned into political movements who vied for leadership. Some people such as the Muslim philosophers, including Ibn Rushd, Ibn Sina, al Farabi and al Kindi even abandoned Islam. In attempting to defend Islam their minds became corrupted in making Islam palatable to the point they became Kafir. It wasn't until the 10th century with the emergence of Imam Ghazali that eventually put an end to the corruption caused by such people. He refuted the thoughts of Aristotle and Plato exposing the deviant thinking of the Muslim philosophers.

10. We should also understand that many Muslims are knowingly advocating the reforming of Islam. Such Muslims have been easily bought by the West and in most cases are smitten by the West and view the whole world from the perspective of the West. Such people range from the extreme to the moderate. Irshad Manji and Ayaan Hirsi Ali (who has left Islam) although both extreme, are both there to appease the non-Muslim audience. However people such as Tariq Ramadan and Ali Gomaa are

actively preparing arguments justifying the reform of Islam. Many national Muslim organisations have also been locked into reforming Islam. However many do so unknowingly. The approach to be taken from Muslims is initially one of outlining to any Muslim who knowingly or unknowingly calls for the reforming of Islam, to show them how their actions aid reform. If such advice is not adhered to then there can be no doubt such an individual wants Islam to be changed. In such a case the thoughts they advocate need to be refuted and they should be named and shamed for defaming the *deen* of Allah. The concept of seventy excuses for a fellow Muslim does not apply here as they have made their intentions very clear. Hence no regard is given to their intention as there actions are directly aiding the changing of Islam. Hence the comments of Tariq Ramadan only have one meaning when he responds to question such as:

"What about apostasy? What happens if you are born and educated a Muslim but then say: I have now decided that Islam is not for me. Would you accept that someone born into a Muslim family has a right to say that they no longer believe, and that families and communities must respect that? He answered "I have been criticised about this in many countries. My view is the same as that of Sufyan Al-Thawri, an 8th-century scholar of Islam, who argued that the Koran does not prescribe death for someone because he or she is changing religion. Neither did the Prophet himself ever perform such an act."[26] Such twisting of Islam aids the West's work and such people need to be named and shamed.

11. There should only be one approach in defending Islam and that is to go on the offensive. For all the attacks on Islam, the security threat it poses, claims of it being ancient, all of this is at a time when Western society and civilisation is falling apart. When President Bush says Islam is intolerant or still stuck in the Stone Age we need to ask why is there one murder every minutes, one rape every 5 minutes, one robbery every 49 seconds, and one burglary every 10 seconds in the US. When the British government accuses

the Muslims of not integrating and being ghettoized we need to ask what Muslims are being encouraged to integrate into, a society where a crime is committed every 24 minutes.[27] We need to ask, for all the noise about the need for democracy and freedom in the Muslim world the state of the West is such that a women gets raped every 3 minutes. We need to ask why do people not give up their seats for the elderly? Why should people not go out after dark? Why do many women feel frightened in the UK, even after they have bolted their front door, have alarms, a dog and neighborhood watch? Why do people as a matter of course need state of the art alarm systems for their cars? Why do I need to overlook my kids playing on the streets? Why do I need to pick up my kids on time after school because of potential pedophiles? We should ask why the UK has the highest rate of teenage pregnancies in Europe and rates of Sexually Transmitted diseases[28] and why are the numbers on the Child Sex Offenders Register over 230,000 with 3,400 pedophiles? Islam does not form the basis of governance in the Muslim world hence it is inevitable problems will exist as there is no coherent way of dealing with them. However in the West where Capitalism is being applied, crime, sexual promiscuity, individualism and civil disorder is rife. Far from being a threat to humanity, the world needs Islam to deliver it from such barbarism.

References

Introduction

[1] BBC News Online, 'EU deplores 'dangerous' Islam jibe,' 27th September 2001, retrieved 30th October 2007, http://news.bbc.co.uk/1/hi/world/europe/1565664.stm

[2] Ahmed H. Al-Rahim (January 2006). "Islam and Liberty", *Journal of Democracy* 17 (1), p. 166-169

[3] Abduh, Muhammad, Al-Manar, *Tafseer* of the Qur'an, Volume 6, al-Maida: (5:44) "and whosoever does not judge by what Allah has revealed, such are the Fasiqun (transgressors), pages 406-409

[4] Alan Cowell, (July 2005) *'Bombings in London: The Prime Minister; Blair Says 'Evil Ideology' Must Be Faced Directly,'* New York Times, retrieved 30th October 2007, http://query.nytimes.com/gst/fullpage.html?res=9C06E7D91F3DF934A25754 C0A9639C8B63

Battle for hearts and Minds

[5] Transcript of Speech by Deputy Secretary of Defence Paul Wolfowitz, Luncheon Press Event in Singapore, May 2002, retrieved October 26th 2007, http://www.defenselink.mil/transcripts/transcript.aspx?transcriptid=3472

[6] National Intelligence Estimate, December 2004, Report of the National Intelligence Councils 2020 project, *'Mapping the Global Future,'* Pg 83-92, retrieved 26th October 2007, http://www.foia.cia.gov/2020/2020.pdf

[7] Chancellor Gordon Brown interview by Andrew Marr, BBC Sunday AM programme, 7th January 2007, full transcript, retrieved 30th October 2007, http://news.bbc.co.uk/1/hi/uk_politics/6241819.stm#us

[8] Bulent Aras and Omer Caha, *'Fethullah Gulen and His Liberal 'Turkish Islam' Movement,'* MERIA Journal, Vol. 4, No. 4, December 2000.

[9] Ken Miichi, *'Islamic Movements in Indonesia,'* IIAS Newsletter, No. 32, November 2003

[10] Der Multikulturalismus hat dem Scharia: Islam in Europa die Tür Geöffnet," NZZ am Sontag, October 2002.

[11] US Department of Defence, Quadrennial Defence Review Report, February 6, 2006, pp. 21–22.

Understanding The battle for hearts and minds

[12] Flemming Rose, 'Why I published Those cartoons,' 19th Feb 2006, Washington Post, retrieved 28th October 2007, http://www.washingtonpost.com/wp-dyn/content/article/2006/02/17/AR2006021702499_pf.html

[13] BBC News Online, *'Straw's veil comments spark anger,'* October 2006, retrieved 27th October 2007, http://news.bbc.co.uk/1/hi/uk_politics/5410472.stm

[14] BBC News Online, *'Blair's concerns over face veils,'* October 17th 2006, retrieved 27th October 2007, http://news.bbc.co.uk/1/hi/uk_politics/6058672.stm

[15] Cherie Blair, Press Conference on Taliban & Women, Tuesday, 20 November 2001, 10:31, Press Release: UK Government

[16] Melanie Phillips, Spectator, September 2002

[17] Salman Rushdie, Aug 2005, *'Muslims unite! A new Reformation will bring your faith into the modern era',* Times, retrieved 24th October 2007,

http://www.timesonline.co.uk/tol/comment/columnists/guest_contributors/article553964.ece

[18] Tariq Ramadan, *'To Be a European Muslim: A Study of Islamic Sources in the European Context,'* Leicester, UK, Islamic Foundation, 1999

[19] Tariq Ramadan, *"An International call for Moratorium on corporal punishment, stoning and the death penalty in the Islamic World,"* April 2005, retrieved 30th October 2007, http://www.tariqramadan.com/article.php3?id_article=264&lang=en

[20] Ali Gomaa, June 2007, *'Fatwas and modernity,'* Dar al-Ifta al-Misriyyah, reproduced in Newsweek Blog, Washington Post (Translated from Arabic), retrieved 24th October   2007,

http://newsweek.washingtonpost.com/onfaith/guestvoices/2007/06/fatwas_an d_modernity.html

[21] retrieved 24th October 2007, http://newsweek.washingtonpost.com/onfaith/muslims_speak_out/2007/07/s heikh_ali_gomah.html

[22] Jonathan Spollen, August 2007, *"Quitting Islam still a matter of life and death,"* The New Zealand Herald, retrieved 24th October 2007, http://www.nzherald.co.nz/category/story.cfm?c_id=301&objectid=10454948

[23] Full interview Transcript, *'Dr Muhammad Abdul Bari: You Ask The Questions,'* The Independent, 29th October 2007, retrieved 31st October 2007, http://news.independent.co.uk/people/profiles/article3106922.ece

Conclusion

[24] Hazrat Mirza Ghulam Ahmad Sahib of Qadian, *'The British Government and Jihad,'* (Government Ungrayzee aur Jihad) Translation by: Imam Kalamazad Mohammed, retrieved 6th November 2007, http://aaiil.org/text/books/mga/britishgovernmentjihad/britishgovernmentjiha d.shtml

[25] Sitara-e-Qaisaria, Roohany Khazaen, Vol. 15, P. 114, Sitara-e-Qaisaria, Pg 3-4 Letter to Queen Victoria, Khutba-Ilhamia

[26] Interview with Tariq Ramadan, by Ehsan Masood, Prospect Magazine, issue 124, July 2006, retrieved 29th October 2007, http://www.prospect-agazine.co.uk/pdfarticle.php?id=7571

[27] Daily Mail "Knife crime figures pile the pressure on Labour," 28th October 2007, retrieved 30th October 2007, http://www.dailymail.co.uk/pages/live/articles/news/news.html?in_article_id= 490135&in_page_id=1770&in_a_source

[28] Mark Townsend, 'Oral sex lessons to cut rates of teenage pregnancy,' May 2004, Guardian, retrieved 7th November 2007
http://education.guardian.co.uk/schools/story/0,,1212831,00.html